D0949773

BLUE NIGHTS

JOAN DIDION

BLUE NIGHTS

ALFRED A. KNOPF   NEW YORK 2011

Grateful acknowledgment is made to the following for permission
to reprint previously published material:

Alfred Music Publishing Co., Inc.: Excerpt from "Hotel California," words
and music by Don Henley, Glenn Frey, and Don Felder, copyright © 1976,
copyright renewed by Cass County Music (BMI), Red Cloud Music (BMI), and
Fingers Music (ASCAP). All print rights for Cass County Music and Red Cloud
Music administered by Warner-Tamerlane Publishing Corp. All rights reserved.
Reprinted by permission of Alfred Music Publishing Co., Inc., on behalf of
Don Henley and Glenn Frey, and Don Felder.

Random House, Inc., and Curtis Brown, Ltd.: "Funeral Blues," copyright
© 1940, copyright renewed 1968 by W. H. Auden; excerpt from "Many Happy
Returns," copyright © 1945, copyright renewed 1973 by W. H. Auden, from
Collected Poems of W. H. Auden by W. H. Auden (currently published by Mod-
ern Library, a division of Random House, Inc.). Reprinted by permission of
Random House, Inc. on behalf of print rights and Curtis Brown, Ltd. on behalf
of audio and electronic rights.

Russell & Volkening, Inc.: Excerpt from "what i thought i'd never lose &
did/what i discovered when i didn't know i cd" by Ntozake Shange, copyright
© 1993 by Ntozake Shange, from *In the Fullness of Time: 32 Women on Life
after 50* (New York: Atria/Simon & Schuster, 2010). Reprinted by permission
of Russell & Volkening as agents for the author.

Library of Congress Cataloging-in-Publication Data
Didion, Joan.
Blue nights / by Joan Didion. — 1st ed.
p. cm.
"This is a Borzoi book."
ISBN 978-0-307-26767-2
1. Didion, Joan.   2. Novelists, American—20th century—Biography.   I. Title.
PS3554.I33Z46 2011
813'.54—dc22
[B]   2011013582

Jacket design by Carol Devine Carson

Manufactured in the United States of America
First Edition

This book is for Quintana

BLUE NIGHTS

1

In certain latitudes there comes a span of time approaching and following the summer solstice, some weeks in all, when the twilights turn long and blue. This period of the blue nights does not occur in subtropical California, where I lived for much of the time I will be talking about here and where the end of daylight is fast and lost in the blaze of the dropping sun, but it does occur in New York, where I now live. You notice it first as April ends and May begins, a change in the season, not exactly a warming—in fact not at all a warming—yet suddenly summer seems near, a possibility, even a promise. You pass a window, you walk to Central Park, you find yourself swimming in the color blue: the actual light is blue, and over the course of an hour or so this blue deepens, becomes more intense even as it darkens and fades, approximates finally the blue of the glass on a clear day at Chartres, or that of the

Cerenkov radiation thrown off by the fuel rods in the pools of nuclear reactors. The French called this time of day "l'heure bleue." To the English it was "the gloaming." The very word "gloaming" reverberates, echoes— the gloaming, the glimmer, the glitter, the glisten, the glamour—carrying in its consonants the images of houses shuttering, gardens darkening, grass-lined rivers slipping through the shadows. During the blue nights you think the end of day will never come. As the blue nights draw to a close (and they will, and they do) you experience an actual chill, an apprehension of illness, at the moment you first notice: the blue light is going, the days are already shortening, the summer is gone. This book is called "Blue Nights" because at the time I began it I found my mind turning increasingly to illness, to the end of promise, the dwindling of the days, the inevitability of the fading, the dying of the brightness. Blue nights are the opposite of the dying of the brightness, but they are also its warning.

2

July 26 2010.

Today would be her wedding anniversary.

Seven years ago today we took the leis from the florist's boxes and shook the water in which they were packed onto the grass outside the Cathedral of St. John the Divine on Amsterdam Avenue. The white peacock spread his fan. The organ sounded. She wove white stephanotis into the thick braid that hung down her back. She dropped a tulle veil over her head and the stephanotis loosened and fell. The plumeria blossom tattooed just below her shoulder showed through the tulle. "Let's do it," she whispered. The little girls in leis and pale dresses skipped down the aisle and walked behind her up to the high altar. After all the words had been said the little girls followed her out the front doors of the cathedral and around past the pea-cocks (the two iridescent blue-and-green peacocks,

the one white peacock) to the Cathedral house. There
were cucumber and watercress sandwiches, a peach-
colored cake from Payard, pink champagne.

Her choices, all.

Sentimental choices, things she remembered.

I remembered them too.

When she said she wanted cucumber and watercress sandwiches at her wedding I remembered her
laying out plates of cucumber and watercress sandwiches on the tables we had set up around the pool
for her sixteenth-birthday lunch. When she said she
wanted leis in place of bouquets at her wedding I
remembered her at three or four or five getting off a
plane at Bradley Field in Hartford wearing the leis she
had been given when she left Honolulu the night
before. The temperature in Connecticut that morning
was six degrees below zero and she had no coat (she
had been wearing no coat when we left Los Angeles for
Honolulu, we had not expected to go on to Hartford)
but she had seen no problem. Children with leis don't
wear coats, she advised me.

Sentimental choices.

On the day of that wedding she got all her sentimental choices except one: she had wanted the little girls
to go barefoot in the cathedral (memory of Malibu, she
was always barefoot in Malibu, she always had splinters from the redwood deck, splinters from the deck

and tar from the beach and iodine for the scratches from the nails in the stairs in between) but the little girls had new shoes for the occasion and wanted to wear them.

MR. AND MRS. JOHN GREGORY DUNNE
REQUEST THE HONOR OF YOUR PRESENCE
AT THE MARRIAGE OF THEIR DAUGHTER,
QUINTANA ROO
TO
MR. GERALD BRIAN MICHAEL
ON SATURDAY THE TWENTY-SIXTH OF JULY
AT TWO O'CLOCK

The stephanotis.

Was that another sentimental choice?

Did she remember the stephanotis?

Is that why she wanted it, is that why she wove it into her braid?

At the house in Brentwood Park in which we lived from 1978 until 1988, a house so determinedly conventional (two stories, center-hall plan, shuttered windows, and a sitting room off every bedroom) as to seem in situ idiosyncratic ("their suburbia house in Brentwood" was how she referred to the house when we bought it, a twelve-year-old establishing that it was not her decision, not her taste, a child claiming the distance all children imagine themselves to need), there was stephanotis growing outside the terrace doors. I would brush the waxy flowers when I went out to the garden. Outside the same doors there were beds of lavender and also mint, a tangle of mint, made lush by a dripping faucet. We moved into that house the summer she was about to start the seventh grade at what was then still the Westlake School for Girls in Holmby Hills. This was like yesterday. We moved out of that house the year she was about to graduate from Barnard. This too was like yesterday. The stephanotis and mint were dead by then, killed when the man who was buying the house insisted that we rid it of termites by tenting it and pumping in Vikane and chloropicrin. At the time this buyer bid on the house he sent us word via the brokers, apparently by way of closing the deal, that he wanted the house because he could picture his daughter marrying in the garden. This was a few weeks before he required us to pump in the Vikane that killed the stephanotis, killed the mint, and also killed the pink magnolia into which the twelve-year-old who took so assiduously removed a view of our suburbia house in Brentwood had until then been able to look from her second-floor sitting-room windows. The termites, I was quite sure, would come back. The pink magnolia, I was also quite sure, would not.

We closed the deal and moved to New York.

Where in fact I had lived before, from the time I was twenty-one and just out of the English Department at Berkeley and starting work at *Vogue* (a segue so profoundly unnatural that when I was asked by the Condé Nast personnel department to name the languages in which I was fluent I could think only of Middle English) until I was twenty-nine and just married.

Where I have lived again since 1988.

Why then do I say I lived much of this time in California?

Why then did I feel so sharp a sense of betrayal when I exchanged my California driver's license for one issued by New York? Wasn't that actually a straightforward enough transaction? Your birthday comes around, your license needs renewing, what difference does it make where you renew it? What difference does it make that you have had this single number on your license since it was assigned to you at age fifteen-and-a-half by the state of California? Wasn't there always an error on that driver's license anyway? An error you knew about? Didn't that license say you were five-foot-two? When you knew perfectly well you were at best—(max height, top height ever, height before you lost a half inch to age)—when you knew perfectly well you were at best five-foot-one-and-three-quarters?

Why did I make so much of the driver's license?

What was that about?

Did giving up the California license say that I would never again be fifteen-and-a-half?

Would I want to be?

Or was the business with the license just one more case of "the apparent inadequacy of the precipitating event"?

I put "the apparent inadequacy of the precipitating event" in quotes because it is not my phrase.

Karl Menninger used it, in *Man Against Himself*, by way of describing the tendency to overreact to what might seem ordinary, even predictable, circumstances: a propensity, Dr. Menninger tells us, common among suicides. He cites the young woman who becomes depressed and kills herself after cutting her hair. He mentions the man who kills himself because he has been advised to stop playing golf, the child who commits suicide because his canary died, the woman who kills herself after missing two trains.

Notice: not one train, *two* trains.

Think that over.

Consider what special circumstances are required before this woman throws it all in.

"In these instances," Dr. Menninger tells us, "the hair, the golf, and the canary had an exaggerated value, so that when they were lost or when there was even a threat that they might be lost, the recoil of severed emotional bonds was fatal."

Yes, clearly, no argument.

"The hair, the golf, and the canary" had each been assigned an exaggerated value (as presumably had the second of those two missed trains), but why? Dr. Menninger himself asks this question, although only rhetorically: "But why should such extravagantly exaggerated over-estimations and incorrect evaluations exist?" Did he imagine that he had answered the question simply by raising it? Did he think that all he had to do was formulate the question and then retreat into a cloud of theoretical psychoanalytic references? Could I seriously have construed changing my driver's license from California to New York as an experience involving "severed emotional bonds"?

Did I seriously see it as loss?

Did I truly see it as separation?

And before we leave this subject of "severed emotional bonds":

The last time I saw the house in Brentwood Park before its title changed hands we stood outside watching the three-level Allied van pull away and turn onto Marlboro Street, everything we then owned, including a Volvo station wagon, already inside and on its way to New York. After the van moved out of sight we walked through the empty house and out across the terrace, a

good-bye moment rendered less tender by the linger-
ing reek of Vikane in the house and the stiff dead
leaves where the pink magnolia and stephanotis had
been. I smelled Vikane even in New York, every time I
unpacked a carton. The next time I was in Los Angeles
and drove past the house it was gone, a teardown, to be
replaced a year or two later by a house marginally big-
ger (a new room over the garage, an additional foot or
two in a kitchen already large enough to accommodate
a square Chickering grand piano that remained mostly
unnoticed) but lacking (for me) the resolute conven-
tionality of the original. Some years later in a Washington bookstore I met the daughter, the one the buyer
had said he could picture marrying in the garden. She
was at school somewhere in Washington (Georgetown?
George Washington?), I was there to give a reading at
Politics and Prose. She introduced herself. I grew up
in your house, she said. Not exactly, I refrained from
saying.

John always said we moved "back" to New York.

I never did.

Brentwood Park was then, New York was now.

Brentwood Park before the Vikane had been a time,
a period, a decade, during which everything had
seemed to connect.

Our suburbia house in Brentwood.

It was exactly that. She called it.

There had been cars, a swimming pool, a garden.

There had been agapanthus, lilies of the Nile, intensely blue starbursts that floated on long stalks. There had been gaura, clouds of tiny white blossoms that became visible at eye level only as the daylight faded.

There had been English chintzes, chinoiserie toile.

There had been a Bouvier des Flandres motionless on the stair landing, one eye open, on guard.

Time passes.

Memory fades, memory adjusts, memory conforms to what we think we remember.

Even memory of the stephanotis in her braid, even memory of the plumeria tattoo showing through the tulle.

It is horrible to see oneself die without children. Napoléon Bonaparte said that.

What greater grief can there be for mortals than to see their children dead. Euripedes said that.

When we talk about mortality we are talking about our children.

I said that.

I think now of that July day at St. John the Divine in 2003 and am struck by how young John and I appeared to be, how well. In actual fact neither of us was in the least well: John had that spring and summer undergone a series of cardiac procedures, most recently the implantation of a pacemaker, the efficacy of which remained in question; I had three weeks before the wedding collapsed on the street and spent the several nights following in a Columbia Presbyterian ICU being transfused for an unexplained gastrointestinal bleed. "You're just going to swallow a little camera," they said in the ICU when they were trying to demonstrate to themselves what was causing the bleed. I recall resisting: since I had never in my life been able to swallow an aspirin it seemed unlikely that I could swallow a camera.

"Of course you can, it's only a *little* camera."

A pause. The attempt at briskness declined into wheedling:

"It's really a *very* little camera."

In the end I did swallow the very little camera, and the very little camera transmitted the desired images, which did not demonstrate what was causing the bleed but did demonstrate that with sufficient sedation anyone could swallow a very little camera. Similarly, in another less than entirely efficient use of high-tech medicine, John could hold a telephone to his heart, dial a number, and get a reading on the pacemaker, which proved, I was told, that at the given instant he dialed the number (although not necessarily before or after) the device was operating.

Medicine, I have had reason since to notice more than once, remains an imperfect art.

Yet all had seemed well when we were shaking the water off the leis onto the grass outside St. John the Divine on July 26 2003. Could you have seen, had you been walking on Amsterdam Avenue and caught sight of the bridal party that day, how utterly unprepared the mother of the bride was to accept what would happen before the year 2003 had even ended? The father of the bride dead at his own dinner table? The bride herself in an induced coma, breathing only on a respirator, not expected by the doctors in the intensive care unit to live the night? The first in a cascade of medical crises that would end twenty months later with her death?

Twenty months during which she would be strong enough to walk unsupported for possibly a month in all?

Twenty months during which she would spend weeks at a time in the intensive care units of four different hospitals?

In all of those intensive care units there were the same blue-and-white printed curtains. In all of those intensive care units there were the same sounds, the same gurgling through plastic tubing, the same dripping from the IV line, the same rales, the same alarms.

In all of those intensive care units there were the same requirements to guard against further infections, the donning of the double gowns, the paper slippers, the surgical cap, the mask, the gloves that pulled on only with difficulty and left a rash that reddened and bled. In all of those intensive care units there was the same racing through the unit when a code was called, the feet hitting the floor, the rattle of the crash cart.

This was never supposed to happen to her, I remember thinking—outraged, as if she and I had been promised a special exemption—in the third of those intensive care units.

By the time she reached the fourth I was no longer invoking this special exemption.

When we talk about mortality we are talking about our children.

I just said that, but what does it mean?

All right, of course I can track it, of course you can track it, another way of acknowledging that our children are hostages to fortune, but when we talk about our children what are we saying? Are we saying what it meant to us to have them? What it meant to us not to have them? What it meant to let them go? Are we talking about the enigma of pledging ourselves to protect the unprotectable? About the whole puzzle of being a parent?

Time passes.

Yes, agreed, a banality, of course time passes.

Then why do I say it, why have I already said it more than once?

Have I been saying it the same way I say I have lived most of my life in California?

Have I been saying it without hearing what I say?

Could it be that I heard it more this way: *Time passes, but not so aggressively that anyone notices*? Or even: *Time passes, but not for me*? Could it be that I did not figure in either the general nature or the permanence of the slowing, the irreversible changes in mind and body, the way in which you wake one summer morning less resilient than you were and by Christmas find your ability to mobilize gone, atrophied, no longer extant? The way in which you live most of your life in California, and then you don't? The way in which your awareness of this passing time—this permanent slowing, this vanishing resilience—multiplies, metastasizes, becomes your very life?

Time passes.

Could it be that I never believed it?

Did I believe the blue nights could last forever?

3

Last spring, 2009, I had some warnings, flags on the track, definite notices of darkening even before the blue nights came.

L'heure bleue. The gloaming.

Not even yet evident when that year's darkening gave its first notices.

The initial such notice was sudden, the ringing telephone you wish you had never answered, the news no one wants to get: someone to whom I had been close since her childhood, Natasha Richardson, had fallen on a ski slope outside Quebec (spring break, a family vacation, a bunny slope, *this was never supposed to happen to her*) and by the time she noticed that she did not feel entirely well she was dying, the victim of an epidural hematoma, a traumatic brain injury. She was the daughter of Vanessa Redgrave and Tony Richardson, who was one of our closest friends in Los Angeles.

The first time I ever saw her she had been maybe thirteen or fourteen, not yet entirely comfortable in her own skin, an uncertain but determined adolescent with a little too much makeup and startlingly white stockings. She had come from London to visit her father at his house on Kings Road in Hollywood, an eccentrically leveled structure that had belonged to Linda Lovelace, the star of *Deep Throat*. Tony had bought the house and proceeded to fill it with light and parrots and whippets. When Tasha arrived from London he had brought her to dinner with us at La Scala. The dinner had not been planned as a party for her arrival but there had happened to be many people her father and we knew at La Scala that night and her father had made it feel like one. She had been pleased. A few years later Quintana had been at the same uncertain age and Tasha, by then seventeen, was spending the summer at Le Nid du Duc, the village her father had invented, an entertainment of his own, a director's conceit, in the hills of the Var above Saint-Tropez.

To say that Tasha was spending the summer at Le Nid du Duc fails to adequately suggest the situation. In fact, by the time John and I arrived in France that summer, Tasha was running Le Nid du Duc, the seventeen-year-old chatelaine of what amounted to a summer-long house party for a floating thirty people. Tasha

was managing the provisioning of the several houses
that made up the compound. Tasha was cooking and
serving, entirely unaided, three meals a day for the
basic thirty as well as for anyone else who happened
up the hill and had a drink and waited for the long
tables under the lime trees to be set—not only cooking
and serving but, as Tony noted in his memoir *The
Long-Distance Runner,* "completely unfazed when told
that there'd be an extra twenty for lunch."

Most astonishingly, at seventeen, Tasha was under-
taking the induction into adult life not only of her
sisters Joely and Katharine but of two Los Angeles
eighth-graders, one of them Quintana, the other Ken-
neth and Kathleen Tynan's daughter Roxana, both
avid to grow up, each determined to misbehave. Tasha
made certain that Quintana and Roxana got to the correct spot on the beach at Saint-Tropez every afternoon,
that summer's correct spot of choice being the Aqua
Club. Tasha made certain that Quintana and Roxana
got a proper introduction to the Italian boys who
trailed them on the beach, a "proper introduction" for
Tasha entailing a meal at the long tables under the
lime trees at Le Nid du Duc. Tasha came up from the
Aqua Club and Tasha did a perfect beurre blanc for
the fish Tony had bought that morning and Tasha
watched Quintana and Roxana mesmerize the Italian
boys into believing that they were dealing not with

fourteen-year-olds last seen in the pastel cotton uniforms of the Westlake and Marlborough Schools for
Girls in Los Angeles but with preternaturally sophisti-
cated undergraduates from UCLA.

And never ever, not once, not ever, did I hear Tasha
blow the whistle on that or on any other of the summer's romantic fables.

Au contraire.

Tasha devised the fables, Tasha wrote the romance.

The last time I ever saw her was a few nights after
she fell on the bunny slope outside Quebec, in a room
at Lenox Hill Hospital in New York, lying as if about to
wake.

She was not about to wake.

She had been flown down from Montreal while her
family met in New York.

When I left the hospital after seeing her there were
photographers outside, waiting for clear camera lines
on the family.

I circled around them onto Park Avenue and walked
on home.

Her first marriage, to the producer Robert Fox, had
taken place in my apartment. She had filled the rooms
with quince blossoms for the ceremony. The blossoms
had eventually fallen but the branches had remained,
brittle and dusty, twigs breaking off, nonetheless still
passing as decorative elements in the living room.

When I walked in from Lenox Hill that night the apartment seemed full of photographs of Tasha and of her father and mother. Her father on location for *The Border,* riding a Panavision camera. Her father on location in Spain, wearing a red windbreaker, directing Melanie Griffith and James Woods on an HBO project he and John and I did together. Her mother backstage at the Booth Theater on West Forty-fifth Street, the year she and I did a play together. Tasha herself, talking to John at one of the long tables she had arranged outside for the wedding dinner on her farm in Millbrook when she was married a second time, this time to Liam Neeson.

She had managed that wedding on the farm as before and after she managed summers at Le Nid du Duc.

She had managed even a priest, a wedding mass. She had kept referring to the priest as "Father Dan." It was only when he stood to actually do the ceremony that I realized that "Father Dan" was Daniel Berrigan, one of the activist Berrigan brothers. It seemed that Daniel Berrigan had been an advisor on Roland Joffé's *The Mission.* It seemed that Liam had played a role in *The Mission.* Tasha had designed the entire event, in other words, as a piece of theater, the very kind of moment Tony liked best in the world. He particularly would have liked Tasha forgetting the wafers for the mass, tearing up long baguettes to pass in their place, but Tony was dead by the day of that wedding.

Tasha died in March 2009.

This was never supposed to happen to her.

On her twenty-first birthday her father had made a film of the lunch he gave in her honor at Linda Lovelace's former house on Kings Road. John had wished her happy birthday, on film. Quintana and Fiona Lewis and Tamara Asseyev had sung "Girls Just Want to Have Fun," on film. After lunch we had untied rafts of white balloons and watched them drift over the Hollywood hills, on film. These are the lines from W. H. Auden that Tony quoted that afternoon as "the best twenty-first birthday wish you can make for anyone":

> *So I wish you first a*
> *Sense of theatre; only*
> *Those who love illusion*
> *And know it will go far—*

Tasha and her father and John and Quintana and the whippets and the parrots and the white balloons, all still there, on film.

I have a copy of the film.

So I wish you first a sense of theatre—

So her father would have said at the wedding in Millbrook.

The second such warning, this one not at all sudden, came in April 2009.

Because I had been showing symptoms of neuritis, or neuropathy, or neurological inflammation (there seemed no general agreement on what to call it), an MRI was done, then an MRA. Neither suggested a definitive reason for the symptoms at hand but images of the Circle of Willis showed evidence of a 4.2 mm by 3.4 mm aneurysm deep in that circle of arteries—the anterior cerebral, the anterior communicating, the internal carotid, the posterior cerebral, and the posterior communicating—at the base of my brain. This finding, the several neurologists who examined the images stressed, was "entirely incidental," had "nothing to do with what we're looking for," and was not even necessarily significant. One of the neurologists ventured that this particular aneurysm "doesn't look ready to blow"; another suggested that "if it does blow, you won't live through it."

This seemed to be offered as encouraging news, and I accepted it as such. At that instant in April 2009 I realized that I was no longer, if I had ever been, afraid to die: I was now afraid not to die, afraid that I might damage my brain (or my heart or my kidneys or my nervous system) and survive, continue living.

Had there been an instant when Tasha was afraid not to die?

Had there been an instant when Quintana was afraid not to die?

Toward the very end, say, for example on the August morning when I walked into the ICU overlooking the river at New York-Cornell and one of what must have been twenty doctors in the unit happened to mention (a point of interest, a teachable moment, Grand Rounds for two students, the husband and the mother of the patient) that they were doing hand compression because the patient could no longer get enough oxygen through the ventilator? Only he did not say "the ventilator," he said "the vent"? And I asked dutifully (the attentive student, up on the vernacular) how long it had been since the patient could get enough oxygen through the vent? And the doctor said it had been at least an hour?

Did I get this all wrong?

Did I misunderstand a key point?

Could they have actually let an hour go by without mentioning to me that her brain had already been damaged by insufficient oxygen?

Put the question another way: what if the attentive student had never asked?

Would they have mentioned it at all?

One further turn of the screw: if I had never asked would she still be alive?

Warehoused somewhere?

No longer sentient but alive, not dead?

What greater grief can there be for mortals than to see their children dead?

Was there an instant when she knew what was in store for her that August morning in the ICU overlooking the river at New York–Cornell?

Did the instant occur that August morning when she was in fact dying?

Or had it occurred years before, when she thought she was?

4

"When Quintana was a little girl, we moved to Malibu, to a house overlooking the Pacific." So began the toast John delivered in the Cathedral house at St. John the Divine on the afternoon she wove the stephanotis into her braid and cut the peach-colored cake from Payard. There were aspects of living in that house overlooking the Pacific that he failed to mention—he failed to mention for example the way the wind would blow down through the canyons and whine under the eaves and lift the roof and coat the white walls with ash from the fireplace, he failed to mention for example the king snakes that dropped from the rafters of the garage into the open Corvette I parked below, he failed to mention for example that king snakes were locally considered a valuable asset because the presence of a king snake in your Corvette was understood to mean (I was never convinced that it did) that you didn't have a rattlesnake in your Corvette—but the following is what he did mention. I can quote what he mentioned exactly because after he mentioned it he wrote it down. He wanted her to have it in his words, his exact memory, in his exact words, of her childhood:

The house didn't have any heat—it had old baseboard heaters, but we were always afraid they'd burn the place up—and so we heated it from this huge walk-in fireplace in the living room. In the morning I'd get up and bring in wood for the day— we used about a cord of wood a week—and then I'd get Q up and make her breakfast and get her ready for school. Joan was trying to finish a book that year, and she would work until two or three in the morning, then have a drink and read some poetry before she came to bed. She always made Q's lunch the night before, and put it in this little blue lunchbox. You should have seen those lunches: they weren't your basic peanut butter and jelly schoolbox lunch. Thin little sandwiches with their crusts cut off, cut into four triangular pieces, kept fresh in Saran Wrap. Or else there would be homemade fried chicken, with little salt and pepper shakers. And for dessert, stemmed strawberries, with sour cream and brown sugar.

So I'd take Q to school, and she'd walk down this steep hill. All the kids wore uniforms—Quintana wore a plaid jumper and a white sweater, and her hair—she was a towhead in that Malibu sun—her hair was in a ponytail. I would watch her disappear down that hill, the Pacific a great big blue background, and I thought it was as beautiful as anything I'd ever seen. So I said to Joan, "You got to see this, babe." The next morning Joan came with us, and when she saw Q disappear down that hill she began to cry.

Today Quintana is walking back up that hill. She's not the towhead with the plaid jumper and the blue lunchbox and the ponytail. She's the Princess Bride—and at the top of that hill stands her Prince. Will you join me please in toasting Gerry and Quintana.

We did.

We joined him in toasting Gerry and Quintana.

We toasted Gerry and Quintana at St. John the Divine and a few hours later, in their absence, at a Chinese restaurant on West Sixty-fifth Street with my brother and his family, we toasted Gerry and Quintana again. We wished them happiness, we wished them health, we wished them love and luck and beautiful children. On that wedding day, July 26, 2003, we

could see no reason to think that such ordinary blessings would not come their way.

Do notice:

We still counted happiness and health and love and
luck and beautiful children as "ordinary blessings."

5

Seven years later.
July 26 2010.

Laid out on a table in front of me today is a group of photographs sent to me only recently but all taken in 1971, summer or fall, in or around the unheated house in Malibu mentioned in the wedding toast. We had moved into that house in January 1971, on a perfectly clear day which turned so foggy that by the time I drove back to the house from a late-day run to the Trancas Market, three-and-a-half miles down the Pacific Coast Highway, I could no longer find the driveway. Since sundown fogs in January and February and March turned out to be as much a given of that stretch of coast as wildfires would be in September and October and November, this disappearance of the driveway was by no means an unusual turn of events: the preferred method for finding it was to hold your breath, avert your mind from the unseeable cliff below, rising two-hundred-some feet from open ocean, and turn left.

Neither the fogs nor the wildfires figure in the photographs.

There are eighteen images.

Each is of the same child at the same age, Quintana at five, her hair, as noted in the wedding toast, bleached by the beach sun. In some she is wearing her plaid uniform jumper, also noted in the toast. In a few she is wearing a cashmere turtleneck sweater I brought her from London when we went that May to do promotion for the European release of *The Panic in Needle Park.* In a few she is wearing a checked gingham dress trimmed in eyelet, a little faded and a little too big for her, the look of a hand-me-down. In others she has on cutoff jeans and a denim Levi jacket with metal studs, a bamboo fishing pole against her shoulder, artfully arranged there (by her) in a spirit less of fishing than of styling, a prop to accessorize the outfit.

The photographs were taken by one of her West Hartford cousins, Tony Dunne, who had arrived on leave from Williams to spend a few months in Malibu. He had been in Malibu only a day or two when she began to lose her first baby tooth. She had noticed the tooth loosening, she had wiggled the tooth, the tooth loosened further. I tried to remember how this situation had been handled in my own childhood. My most coherent memory involved my mother tying a piece of thread around the loose tooth, attaching the thread to a doorknob, and slamming the door. I tried this. The tooth stayed fixed in place. She cried. I grabbed the car keys and screamed for Tony: tying the thread to the doorknob had so exhausted my aptitude for improvisational caretaking that my sole remaining thought was to get her to the emergency room at UCLA Medical Center, thirty-some miles into town. Tony, who grew up with three siblings and many cousins, tried without success to convince me that UCLA Medical Center might be overkill. "Just let me try just this one thing first," he said finally, and pulled the tooth.

The next time a tooth got loose she pulled it herself. I had lost my authority.

Was I the problem? Was I always the problem?

In the note Tony included when he sent the photographs a few months ago he said that each image represented something he had seen in her. In some she is melancholy, large eyes staring directly into the lens. In others she is bold, daring the camera. She covers her mouth with her hand. She obscures her eyes with a polka-dotted cotton sun hat. She marches through the wash at the edge of the sea. She bites her lip as she swings from an oleander branch.

A few of these photographs are familiar to me.

A copy of one of them, one in which she is wearing

the cashmere turtleneck sweater I bought her in London, is framed on my desk in New York.

There is also on my desk in New York a framed photograph she herself took one Christmas on Barbados: the rocks outside the rented house, the shallow sea, the wash of surf. I remember the Christmas she took that picture. We had arrived on Barbados at night. She had gone immediately to bed and I had sat outside listening to a radio and trying to locate a line I believed to be from Claude Lévi-Strauss's *Tristes Tropiques* but was never able to find: "The tropics are not exotic, they are merely out of date." At some point after she went to sleep news had come on the radio: since our arrival on Barbados the United States had invaded Panama. When the first light came I had woken her with this necessary, or so it seemed to me, information. She had covered her face with the sheet, clearly indicating no interest in pursuing the topic. I had nonetheless pressed it. I knew "exactly yesterday" we were going to invade Panama last night, she had said. I asked how she had known "exactly yesterday" we were going to invade Panama last night. Because all the SIPA photographers were stopping by the office yesterday, she said, picking up credentials for the Panama invasion. SIPA was the photo agency for which she then worked. She had again burrowed beneath the sheet. I did not ask why she had not thought the invasion of Panama worth a mention on the five-hour flight down. *"For Mom and Dad,"* the inscription on the photograph reads. *"Try to imagine the seductive sea if you can, love XX, Q."*

She had known exactly yesterday we were going to invade Panama last night.

The tropics were not exotic, they were merely out of date.

Try to imagine the seductive sea if you can.

Even in those Malibu photographs which are unfamiliar, I recognize certain elements: the improvised end table by a chair in the living room, one of my mother's "Craftsman" dinner knives on the table we identified as "Aunt Kate's," the straightbacked wooden Hitchcock chairs my mother-in-law had painted black-and-gold to send to us from Connecticut.

The oleander branch on which she swings is familiar, the curve of the beach on which she kicks through the wash is familiar.

The clothes of course are familiar.

I had for a while seen them every day, washed them, hung them to blow in the wind on the clotheslines outside my office window.

I wrote two books watching her clothes blow on those lines.

Brush your teeth, brush your hair, shush I'm working.

So read the list of "Mom's Sayings" that she posted one day in the garage, an artifact of the "club" she had started with a child who lived down the beach.

What remained until now unfamiliar, what I recognize in the photographs but failed to see at the time they were taken, are the startling depths and shallows of her expressions, the quicksilver changes of mood.

How could I have missed what was so clearly there to be seen?

Did I not read the poem she brought home that year from the school on the steep hill? The school to which she wore the plaid uniform jumper and carried the blue lunchbox? The school to which John watched her walk every morning and thought it was as beautiful as anything he had ever seen?

"The World," this poem is called, and I recognize her careful printing, quixotically executed on a narrow strip of construction paper fourteen inches long but only two inches wide. I see that careful printing every day: the strip of construction paper is now framed on a wall behind my kitchen in New York, along with a few other mementos of the period: a copy of Karl Shapiro's "California Winter," torn from *The New Yorker;* a copy of Pablo Neruda's "A Certain Weariness," typed by me on one of the several dozen Royal manuals my father had bought (along with a few mess halls, a fire tower, and the regulation khaki Ford jeep on which I learned to drive) at a government auction; a postcard from Bogotá, sent by John and me to Quintana in Malibu; a photograph showing the coffee table in the beach house living room after dinner, the candles burning down and the silver baby cups filled with santolina; a mimeographed notice from the Topanga–Las Virgenes Fire District instructing residents of the district what to do "when the fire comes."

Do note: not "*if* the fire comes."

When the fire comes.

No one at the Topanga–Las Virgenes Fire District was talking about what most people see when they hear the words "brush fire," a few traces of smoke and an occasional lick of flame: at the Topanga–Las Virgenes Fire District they were talking about fires that burned on twenty-mile fronts and spotted ahead twelve-foot flames as they moved.

This was not forgiving territory: consider finding the driveway.

Also consider "The World" itself, its eccentric strip of construction paper and careful printing obscuring one side of the mimeographed notice from the Topanga–Las Virgenes Fire District. Since the choices made by the careful printer may or may not have meaning, I give you the text of "The World" with her spacing, her single misspelling:

THE
WORLD

The world
Has nothing
But morning
And night
It has no
Day or lunch
So this world
Is poor and desertid.
This is some
Kind of an
Island with
Only three
Houses on it
In these
Families are
2,1,2, people
In each house
So 2,1,2 make
Only 5 people
On this
Island.

In point of fact the beach on which we lived, our personal "some Kind of an Island," did have "Only three Houses on it," or, more correctly, it had only three houses that were occupied year-round. One of these three houses was owned by Dick Moore, a cinematographer who, when he was not on a location, lived there with his two daughters, Marina and Tita. It was Tita Moore who started the club with Quintana that entailed posting "Mom's Sayings" in our garage. Tita and Quintana also had an entrepreneurial enterprise, "the soap factory," the business mission of which was to melt down and reshape all remaining bars of the gardenia-scented I. Magnin soap I used to order by the box and sell the result to passers-by on the beach. Since both ends of this beach were submerged by the tide, no more than two or three passers-by would actually materialize during the soap factory's operating hours, enabling me to buy back my own I. Magnin soap, reconfigured from pristine ivory ovals into gray blobs. I have no memory of the other "Families" in these houses, but in our own I would have said that there were not "2, 1, 2, people" but "3 people."

Possibly Quintana saw our personal "some Kind of an Island" differently.

Possibly she had reason to.

Brush your teeth, brush your hair, shush I'm working.

Once when we were living in the beach house we came home to find that she had placed a call to what was known familiarly on our stretch of the coast as "Camarillo." Camarillo was at that time a state psychiatric facility twenty-some miles north of us in Ventura County, the hospital in which Charlie Parker once detoxed and then memorialized in "Relaxin' at Camarillo," the institution sometimes said to have provided inspiration to the Eagles for "Hotel California."

She had called Camarillo, she advised us, to find out what she needed to do if she was going crazy.

She was five years old.

On another occasion we came home to the beach house and found that she had placed a call to Twentieth Century–Fox.

She had called Twentieth Century–Fox, she explained, to find out what she needed to do to be a star.

Again, she was five years old, maybe six.

Tita Moore is dead now, she died before Quintana did.

Dick Moore is dead now too, he died last year.

Marina called me recently.

I do not remember what Marina and I talked about but I know we did not talk about the club with "Mom's Sayings" in the garage and I know we did not talk about the soap factory and I know we did not talk about how the ends of the beach got submerged by the tide.

I say this because I do not believe that either Marina or I could have managed such a conversation.

> *Relax, said the night man—*
> *We are programmed to receive—*
> *You can check out any time you like—*
> *But you can never leave—*

So goes the lyric to "Hotel California."

Depths and shallows, quicksilver changes.

She was already a person. I could never afford to see that.

6

What about the "Craftsman" dinner knife of my mother's?

The "Craftsman" dinner knife on Aunt Kate's table, the one I recognize in the photographs? Was it the same "Craftsman" dinner knife that dropped through the redwood slats of the deck into the iceplant on the slope? The same "Craftsman" dinner knife that stayed lost in the iceplant until the blade was pitted and the handle scratched? The knife we found only when we were correcting the drainage on the slope in order to pass the geological inspection required to sell the house and move to Brentwood Park? The knife I saved to pass on to her, a memento of the beach, of her grandmother, of her childhood?

I still have the knife.

Still pitted, still scratched.

I also still have the baby tooth her cousin Tony pulled, saved in a satin-lined jeweler's box, along with the baby teeth she herself eventually pulled and three loose pearls.

The baby teeth were to have been hers as well.

7

In fact I no longer value this kind of memento.

I no longer want reminders of what was, what got broken, what got lost, what got wasted.

There was a period, a long period, dating from my childhood until quite recently, when I thought I did.

A period during which I believed that I could keep people fully present, keep them with me, by preserving their mementos, their "things," their totems.

The detritus of this misplaced belief now fills the drawers and closets of my apartment in New York. There is no drawer I can open without seeing something I do not want, on reflection, to see. There is no closet I can open with room left for the clothes I might actually want to wear. In one closet that might otherwise be put to such use I see, instead, three old Burberry raincoats of John's, a suede jacket given to Quintana by the mother of her first boyfriend, and an

angora cape, long since moth-eaten, given to my
mother by my father not long after World War Two. In
another closet I find a chest of drawers and perilously
stacked assortment of boxes. I open one of the boxes. I
find photographs taken by my grandfather when he
was a mining engineer in the Sierra Nevada in the
early years of the twentieth century. In another of the
boxes I find the scraps of lace and embroidery that my
mother had salvaged from her own mother's boxes of
mementos.

The jet beads.

The ivory rosaries.

The objects for which there is no satisfactory resolution.

In the third of the boxes I find skein after skein of
needlepoint yarn, saved in the eventuality that reme-
dial stitches might ever be required on a canvas com-
pleted and given away in 2001. In the chest of drawers
I find papers written by Quintana when she was still at
the Westlake School for Girls: the research study on
stress, the analysis of Angel Clare's role in *Tess of the
d'Urbervilles.* I find her Westlake summer uniforms, I
find her navy-blue gym shorts. I find the blue-and-
white pinafore she wore for volunteering at St. John's
Hospital in Santa Monica. I find the black wool challis
dress I bought her when she was four at Bendel's on
West Fifty-seventh Street. When I bought that black

wool challis dress Bendel's was still on West Fifty-seventh Street. It was that long ago. Bendel's became after Geraldine Stutz stopped running it just another store but when it was still on West Fifty-seventh Street and I bought that dress it was special, it was everything I wanted either one of us to wear, it was all Holly's Harp chiffon and lettuce edges and sizes zero and two.

Other objects for which there is no satisfactory resolution.

I continue opening boxes.

I find more faded and cracked photographs than I want ever again to see.

I find many engraved invitations to the weddings of people who are no longer married.

I find many mass cards from the funerals of people whose faces I no longer remember.

In theory these mementos serve to bring back the moment.

In fact they serve only to make clear how inadequately I appreciated the moment when it was here.

How inadequately I appreciated the moment when it was here is something else I could never afford to see.

8

Her depths and shallows, her quicksilver changes. Of course they were not allowed to remain just that, depths, shallows, quicksilver changes.

Of course they were eventually assigned names, a "diagnosis." The names kept changing. Manic depression for example became OCD and OCD was short for obsessive-compulsive disorder and obsessive-compulsive disorder became something else, I could never remember just what but in any case it made no difference because by the time I did remember there would be a new name, a new "diagnosis." I put the word "diagnosis" in quotes because I have not yet seen that case in which a "diagnosis" led to a "cure," or in fact to any outcome other than a confirmed, and therefore an enforced, debility.

Yet another demonstration of medicine as an imperfect art.

She was depressed. She was anxious. Because she was depressed and because she was anxious she drank too much. This was called medicating herself. Alcohol has its own well-known defects as a medication for depression but no one has ever suggested—ask any doctor—that it is not the most effective anti-anxiety agent yet known. This would seem a fairly straight-forward dynamic, yet, once medicalized—once the depths and shallows and quicksilver changes had been assigned names—it appeared not to be. We went through many diagnoses, many conditions that got called by many names, before the least programmatic among her doctors settled on one that seemed to apply. The name of the condition that seemed to apply was this: "borderline personality disorder." "Patients with this diagnosis are a complex mixture of strengths and weaknesses that confuse the diagnostician and frus-trate the psychotherapist." So notes a 2001 *New England Journal of Medicine* review of John G. Gun-derson's *Borderline Personality Disorder: A Clinical Guide.* "Such patients may seem charming, composed, and psychologically intact one day and collapse into suicidal despair the next." The review continues: "Impulsivity, affective lability, frantic efforts to avoid abandonment, and identity diffusion are all hall-marks."

I had seen most of these hallmarks.

I had seen the charm, I had seen the composure, I had seen the suicidal despair.

I had seen her wishing for death as she lay on the floor of her sitting room in Brentwood Park, the sitting room from which she had been able to look into the pink magnolia. *Let me just be in the ground,* she had kept sobbing. *Let me just be in the ground and go to sleep.*

I had seen the impulsivity.

I had seen the "affective lability," the "identity diffusion."

What I had not seen, or what I had in fact seen but had failed to recognize, were the "frantic efforts to avoid abandonment."

How could she have ever imagined that we could abandon her?

Had she no idea how much we needed her?

I recently read for the first time several fragments of what she had referred to at the time she wrote them as "the novel I'm writing just to show you." She must have been thirteen or fourteen when this project occurred to her. "Some of the events are based on the truth and the others are fictitious," she advises the reader at the outset. "The names have not yet been definitively changed." The protagonist in these fragments, also fourteen and also named Quintana (although sometimes referred to by other names, presumably trials for the definitive changes to come), believes she may be pregnant. She consults, in a plot point that seems specifically crafted to "confuse the diagnostician and frustrate the psychotherapist," her pediatrician. The pediatrician advises her that she must tell her parents. She does so. Her idea of how her parents would respond seems, like the entire rest of the plot point involving the pregnancy, confused, a fantasy, a manifestation of what might be extreme emotional distress or might be no more than narrative inventiveness: "They said that they would provide the abortion but after that they did not even care about her any more. She could live in their suburbia house in Brentwood, but they didn't even care what she did any more. That was fine in her book. Her father had a bad temper, but it showed that they cared very much about their only child. Now, they didn't even care any more. Quintana would lead her life any way she wanted."

At this point the fragment skids to an abrupt close: "On the next pages you will find out why and how Quintana died and her friends became complete burnouts at the age of eighteen."

So ended the novel she was writing just to show us.

Show us what?

Show us that she could write a novel?

Show us why and how she would die?

Show us what she believed our reaction would be?

Now, they didn't even care any more.

No.

She had no idea how much we needed her.

How could we have so misunderstood one another?

Had she chosen to write a novel because we wrote novels? Had it been one more obligation pressed on her? Had she felt it as a fear? Had we?

What follows are notes I made about a figure who at an earlier point had populated her nightmares, a fantast she called The Broken Man and described so often and with such troubling specificity that I was frequently moved to check for him on the terrace outside her second-floor windows. "He has on a blue work shirt, like a repair man," she repeatedly told me. "Short sleeves. He has his name always on his shirt. On the right-hand side. His name is David, Bill, Steve, one of those common names. I would guess this man is maybe age fifty to fifty-nine. Cap like a Dodger cap, navy blue, *GULF* on it. Brown belt, navy-blue pants, black really shiny shoes. And he talks to me in a really deep voice: *Hello, Quintana. I'm going to lock you here in the garage.* After I became five I never ever dreamed about him."

David, Bill, Steve, one of those common names?
Name always on his shirt? On the right-hand side?
Cap like a Dodger cap, navy blue, *GULF* on it?

After she became five she never ever dreamed
about him?

It was when she said "I would guess this man is
maybe age fifty to fifty-nine" that I realized my fear of
The Broken Man to be as unquestioning as her own.

9

O n this question of fear.

When I began writing these pages I believed their subject to be children, the ones we have and the ones we wish we had, the ways in which we depend on our children to depend on us, the ways in which we encourage them to remain children, the ways in which they remain more unknown to us than they do to their most casual acquaintances; the ways in which we remain equally opaque to them.

The ways in which for example we write novels "just to show" each other.

The ways in which our investments in each other remain too freighted ever to see the other clear.

The ways in which neither we nor they can bear to contemplate the death or the illness or even the aging of the other.

As the pages progressed it occurred to me that their

actual subject was not children after all, at least not children *per se,* at least not children *qua* children: their actual subject was this refusal even to engage in such contemplation, this failure to confront the certainties of aging, illness, death.

This fear.

Only as the pages progressed further did I understand that the two subjects were the same.

When we talk about mortality we are talking about our children.

Hello, Quintana. I'm going to lock you here in the garage.

After I became five I never ever dreamed about him.

Once she was born I was never not afraid.

I was afraid of swimming pools, high-tension wires, lye under the sink, aspirin in the medicine cabinet, The Broken Man himself. I was afraid of rattlesnakes, riptides, landslides, strangers who appeared at the door, unexplained fevers, elevators without operators and empty hotel corridors. The source of the fear was obvious: it was the harm that could come to her. A question: if we and our children could in fact see the other clear would the fear go away? Would the fear go away for both of us, or would the fear go away only for me?

10

She was born in the first hour of the third day of March, 1966, at St. John's Hospital in Santa Monica. We were told that we could adopt her late the afternoon of the same day, March third, when Blake Watson, the obstetrician who delivered her, called the house at Portuguese Bend in which we then lived, forty-some miles down the coast from Santa Monica. I was taking a shower and burst into tears when John came into the bathroom to report what Blake Watson had said. "I have a beautiful baby girl at St. John's," is what he had said. "I need to know if you want her." The baby's mother, he had said, was from Tucson. She had been staying with relatives in California for the birth of the baby. An hour later we stood outside the window of the nursery at St. John's looking at an infant with fierce dark hair and rosebud features. The beads on her wrist spelled out not her name but "N.I.," for

"No Information," which was the hospital's response to any questions that might be asked about a baby being placed for adoption. One of the nurses had tied a pink ribbon in the fierce dark hair. "Not *that* baby," John would repeat to her again and again in the years that followed, reenacting the nursery scene, the recommended "choice" narrative, the moment when, of all the babies in the nursery, we picked her. "Not *that* baby . . . *that* baby. The baby with the ribbon."

"Do *that baby*," she would repeat in return, a gift to us, an endorsement of our wisdom in opting to follow the recommended choice narrative. The choice narrative is no longer universally favored by professionals of child care, but it was in 1966. "Do it again. Do the baby with the ribbon."

And later: "Do the part about Dr. Watson calling." Blake Watson was already a folk figure in this recital.

And then: "Tell the part about the shower."

Even the shower had become part of the recommended choice narrative.

March 3, 1966.

After we left St. John's that night we stopped in Beverly Hills to tell John's brother Nick and his wife, Lenny. Lenny offered to meet me at Saks in the morning to buy a layette. She was taking ice from a crystal bucket, making celebratory drinks. Making celebratory drinks was what we did in our family to mark any unusual, or for that matter any usual, occasion. In retrospect we all drank more than we needed to drink but this did not occur to any of us in 1966. Only when I read my early fiction, in which someone was always downstairs making a drink and singing "Big Noise blew in from Winnetka," did I realize how much we all drank and how little thought we gave to it. Lenny added more ice to my glass and took the crystal bucket to the kitchen for a refill. "Saks because if you spend eighty dollars they throw in the bassinette," she added as she went.

I took the glass and put it down.

I had not considered the need for a bassinette.

I had not considered the need for a layette.

The baby with the fierce dark hair stayed that night and the next two in the nursery at St. John's and at some point during each of those nights I woke in the house at Portuguese Bend to the same chill, hearing the surf break on the rocks below, dreaming that I had forgotten her, left her asleep in a drawer, gone into town for dinner or a movie and made no provision for the infant who could even then be waking alone and hungry in the drawer in Portuguese Bend.

Dreaming in other words that I had failed.

Been given a baby and failed to keep her safe.

When we think about adopting a child, or for that matter about having a child at all, we stress the "blessing" aspect.

We omit the instant of the sudden chill, the "what-if," the free fall into certain failure.

What if I fail to take care of this baby?

What if this baby fails to thrive, what if this baby fails to love me?

And worse yet, worse by far, so much worse as to be unthinkable, except I did think it, everyone who has ever waited to bring a baby home thinks it: *what if I fail to love this baby?*

March 3, 1966.

Until that instant when Lenny mentioned the bassinette it had all happened very fast. Until the bassinette it had all seemed casual, even blithe, not different in spirit from the Jax jerseys and printed cotton Lilly Pulitzer shifts we were all wearing that year: on New Year's weekend 1966 John and I had gone to Cat Harbor, on the far side of Catalina Island, on Morty Hall's boat. Morty Hall was married to Diana Lynn. Diana was a close friend of Lenny's. At some point on the boat that weekend (presumably at a point, given the drift of the excursion, when we were having or thinking about having or making or thinking about making a drink) I had mentioned to Diana that I was trying to have a baby. Diana had said I should talk to Blake Watson. Blake Watson had delivered her and Morty's four children. Blake Watson had also delivered the adopted daughter of Howard and Lou Erskine, old friends of Nick and Lenny's (Howard had gone to Williams with Nick) who happened to be on the boat that weekend. Maybe because the Erskines were there or maybe because I had mentioned wanting a baby or maybe because we had all had the drink we were thinking about having, the topic of adoption had entered the ether. Diana herself, it seemed, had been adopted, but this information had been withheld from her until she was twenty-one and it had become necessary for some financial reason that she know. Her adoptive parents had handled the situation by revealing the secret to (this had not seemed unusual at the time) Diana's agent. Diana's agent had handled the situation by taking Diana to lunch at (nor at the time had this) the Beverly Hills Hotel. Diana got the news in the Polo Lounge. She could remember fleeing into the bougainvillea around the bungalows, screaming.

That was all.

Yet the next week I was meeting Blake Watson.

When he called us from the hospital and asked if we

wanted the beautiful baby girl there had been no hesitation: we wanted her. When they asked us at the hospital what we would call the beautiful baby girl there had been no hesitation: we would call her Quintana Roo. We had seen the name on a map when we were in Mexico a few months before and promised each other that if ever we had a daughter (dreamy speculation, no daughter had been in the offing) Quintana Roo would be her name. The place on the map called Quintana Roo was still not yet a state but a territory.

The place on the map called Quintana Roo was still frequented mainly by archaeologists, herpetologists, and bandits. The institution that became spring break in Cancún did not yet exist. There were no bargain flights. There was no Club Med.

The place on the map called Quintana Roo was still terra incognita.

As was the infant in the nursery at St. John's.

L'adoptada, she came to be called in the household. The adopted one.

M'ija she was also called. My daughter.

Adoption, I was to learn although not immediately, is hard to get right.

As a concept, even what was then its most widely approved narrative carried bad news: if someone "chose" you, what does that tell you?

Doesn't it tell you that you were available to be "chosen"?

Doesn't it tell you, in the end, that there are only two people in the world?

The one who "chose" you?

And the other who didn't?

Are we beginning to see how the word "abandonment" might enter the picture? Might we not make efforts to avoid such abandonment? Might not such efforts be characterized as "frantic"? Do we want to ask ourselves what follows? Do we need to ask ourselves what words come next to mind? Isn't one of those words "fear"? Isn't another of those words "anxiety"?

Terra incognita, as I had seen it until then, meant free of complications.

That terra incognita could present its own complications had never occurred to me.

11

On the day her adoption became legal, a hot September afternoon in 1966, we took her from the courthouse in downtown Los Angeles to lunch at The Bistro in Beverly Hills. At the courthouse she had been the only baby up for adoption; the other prospective adoptees that day were all adults, petitioning to adopt one another for one or another tax advantage. At The Bistro, too, more predictably, she was the only baby. *Qué hermosa*, the waiters crooned. *Qué chula*. They gave us the corner banquette usually saved for Sidney Korshak, a gesture the import of which would be clear only to someone who had lived in that particular community at that particular time. "Let's just say a nod from Korshak, and the Teamsters change management," the producer Robert Evans would later write by way of explaining who Sidney Korshak was. "A nod from Korshak, and Vegas shuts down. A nod from Korshak, and the Dodgers suddenly can play night baseball." The waiters placed her carrier on the table between us. She was wearing a blue-and-white dotted organdy dress. She was not quite seven months old. As far as I was concerned this lunch at Sidney Korshak's banquette at The Bistro was the happy ending to the choice narrative. We had chosen, the beautiful baby girl had accepted our choice, no natural parent had stood up at the courthouse and exercised his or her absolute legal right under the California law covering private adoptions to simply say no, she's mine, I want her back.

The issue, as I preferred to see it, was now closed.

The fear was now gone.

She was ours.

What I would not realize for another few years was that I had never been the only person in the house to feel the fear.

What if you hadn't answered the phone when Dr. Watson called, she would suddenly say. *What if you hadn't been home, what if you couldn't meet him at the hospital, what if there'd been an accident on the freeway, what would happen to me then?*

Since I had no adequate answer to these questions, I refused to consider them.

She considered them.

She lived with them.

And then she didn't.

"You have your wonderful memories," people said later, as if memories were solace. Memories are not. Memories are by definition of times past, things gone. Memories are the Westlake uniforms in the closet, the faded and cracked photographs, the invitations to the weddings of the people who are no longer married, the mass cards from the funerals of the people whose faces you no longer remember. Memories are what you no longer want to remember.

12

Sidney Korshak, 88, Dies; Fabled Fixer for the Chicago Mob:

So read the headline on Sidney Korshak's obituary, when he died in 1996, in *The New York Times.* "It was a tribute to Sidney Korshak's success that he was never indicted, despite repeated Federal and state investigations," the obituary continued. "And the widespread belief that he had in fact committed the very crimes the authorities could never prove made him an indispensable ally of leading Hollywood producers, corporate executives and politicians."

Thirty years before Morty Hall had declared on principle that he and Diana would refuse to go to any party given by Sidney Korshak.

I remember Morty and Diana arguing heatedly at dinner one night over this entirely hypothetical point.

Morty and Diana and the heated argument at dinner

about whether or not to refuse to go to a party given by
Sidney Korshak are, I have to conclude, what people
mean when they mention my wonderful memories.

I recently saw Diana in an old commercial, one of
those curiosities that turn up on YouTube. She is wearing a pale mink stole, draping herself over the hood of
an Olds 88. In her smoky voice, she introduces the
Olds 88 as "the hottest number I know." The Olds 88
at this point begins to talk to Diana, mentioning its
own "rocket engine" and "hydra-matic drive." Diana
wraps herself in the pale mink stole. "This is *great*,"
she replies to the Olds 88, again in the smoky voice.

It occurs to me that Diana does not sound in this
Olds 88 commercial as if she would necessarily refuse
to go to a party given by Sidney Korshak.

It also occurs to me that no one who now comes
across this Olds 88 commercial on YouTube would
know who Sidney Korshak was, or for that matter who
Diana was, or even what an Olds 88 was.

Time passes.

Diana is dead now. She died in 1971, at age forty-
five, of a cerebral bleed.

She had collapsed after a wardrobe fitting for a
picture she was due to start in a few days, the third
lead, after Tuesday Weld and Anthony Perkins, in
Play It As It Lays, for which John and I had written the
screenplay and in which she was replaced by Tammy

Grimes. The last time I saw her was in an ICU at Cedars-Sinai in Los Angeles. Lenny and I had gone together to Cedars to see her. The next time Lenny and I were in an ICU at Cedars together it was to see her and Nick's daughter Dominique, who had been strangled outside her house in Hollywood. "She looks even worse than Diana did," Lenny whispered when she saw Dominique, her intake of breath so sudden that I could barely hear her. I knew what Lenny was saying. Lenny was saying that Diana had not lived. Lenny was saying that Dominique was not going to live. I knew this—I suppose I had known it from the time the police officer who called identified himself as "Homicide"—but did not want to hear anyone say it. I ran into one of Diana's daughters a few months ago, in New York. We had lunch in the neighborhood. Diana's daughter remembered that we had last seen each other when Diana was still alive and living in New York and I had brought Quintana to play with her daughters. We promised to keep in touch. It occurred to me as I walked home that I had seen too many people for the last time in one or another ICU.

13

For everything there is a season.

Ecclesiastes, yes, but I think first of The Byrds, "Turn Turn Turn."

I think first of Quintana Roo sitting on the bare hardwood floors of the house on Franklin Avenue and the waxed terra-cotta tiles of the house in Malibu listening to The Byrds on eight-track.

The Byrds and The Mamas and the Papas, "Do You Wanna Dance?"

"I wanna dance," she would croon back to the eight-track.

For everything there is a season. *I'd miss having the seasons,* people from New York like to say by way of indicating the extraordinary pride they take in not living in Southern California. In fact Southern California does have seasons (it has for example "fire season" or "the season when the fire comes," and it also has "the

season when the rain comes," but such Southern California seasons, arriving as they do so theatrically as to
seem strokes of random fate, do not inexorably suggest
the passage of time. Those other seasons, the ones so
prized on the East Coast, do. Seasons in Southern California suggest violence, but not necessarily death.
Seasons in New York—the relentless dropping of the
leaves, the steady darkening of the days, the blue
nights themselves—suggest only death. For my having
a child there was a season. That season passed. I have
not yet located the season in which I do not hear her
crooning back to the eight-track.

I still hear her crooning back to the eight-track.

I wanna dance.

The same way I still see the stephanotis in her
braid, the plumeria tattoo through her veil.

Something else I still see from that wedding day at
St. John the Divine: the bright red soles on her shoes.

She was wearing Christian Louboutin shoes, pale
satin with bright red soles.

You saw the red soles when she kneeled at the altar.

14

Before she was born we had been planning a trip to Saigon.

We had assignments from magazines, we had credentials, we had everything we needed.

Including, suddenly, a baby.

That year, 1966, during which the American military presence in Vietnam would reach four hundred thousand and American B-52s had begun bombing the North, was not widely considered an ideal year to take an infant to Southeast Asia, yet it never occurred to me to abandon or even adjust the plan. I even went so far as to shop for what I imagined we would need: Donald Brooks pastel linen dresses for myself, a flowered Porthault parasol to shade the baby, as if she and I were about to board a Pan Am flight and disembark at *Le Cercle Sportif.*

In the end this trip to Saigon did not take place,

although its cancellation was by no means based on what might have seemed the obvious reason—we canceled, it turned out, because John had to finish the book he had contracted to write about César Chávez and his National Farm Workers Association and the DiGiorgio grape strike in Delano—and I mention Saigon at all only by way of suggesting the extent of my misconceptions about what having a child, let alone adopting one, might actually entail.

How could I not have had misconceptions?

I had been handed this perfect baby, out of the blue, at St. John's Hospital in Santa Monica. She could not have been more exactly the baby I wanted. In the first place she was beautiful. *Hermosa, chula.* Strangers stopped me on the street to tell me so. "I have a beautiful baby girl at St. John's," Blake Watson had said, and he did. Everyone sent dresses, an homage to the beautiful baby girl. There the dresses were in her closet, sixty of them (I counted them, again and again), immaculate little wisps of batiste and Liberty lawn on miniature wooden hangers. The miniature wooden hangers, too, were a gift to the beautiful baby girl, another homage from her instantly acquired relatives, besotted aunts and uncles and cousins in West Hartford (John's family) and Sacramento (mine). I recall changing her dress four times on the afternoon the State of California social worker made her mandated visit to observe the candidate for adoption in the home environment.

We sat on the lawn.

The candidate for adoption played at our feet.

I did not mention to the social worker that Saigon had until recently figured in the candidate's future.

Nor did I mention that current itineraries called for her to sojourn instead at the Starlight Motel in Delano.

Arcelia, who cleaned the house and laundered the wisps of batiste, busied herself watering, as anticipated.

"As anticipated" because I had prepped Arcelia for the visit.

The thought of an unstructured encounter between Arcelia and a State of California social worker had presented spectral concerns from the outset, imagined scenarios that kept me awake at four in the morning and only multiplied as the date of the visit approached: what if the social worker were to notice that Arcelia spoke only Spanish? What if the social worker were to happen into the question of Arcelia's papers? What would the social worker put in her report if she divined that I was entrusting the perfect baby to an undocumented alien?

The social worker remarked, in English, on the fine weather.

I tensed, fearing a trap.

Arcelia smiled, beatific, and continued watering.

I relaxed.

At which point Arcelia, no longer beatific but dra-
matic, flung the hose across the lawn and snatched up
Quintana, screaming *"Víbora!"*

The social worker lived in Los Angeles, she had to
know what *víbora* meant, *víbora* in Los Angeles meant
snake and snake in Los Angeles meant rattlesnake. I
was relatively certain that the rattlesnake was a fantasy but I nonetheless guided Arcelia and Quintana
inside, then turned to the social worker. It's a game, I
lied. Arcelia pretends she sees a snake. We all laugh.
Because you can see. There is no snake.

There could be no snake in Quintana Roo's garden.

Only later did I see that I had been raising her as
a doll.

She would never have faulted me for that.

She would have seen it as a logical response to my
having been handed, out of the blue at St. John's Hospital in Santa Monica, the beautiful baby girl, herself.
At the house after her christening at St. Martin of
Tours Catholic Church in Brentwood we had watercress sandwiches and champagne and later, for anyone still around at dinner time, fried chicken. The
house we were renting that spring belonged to Sara
Mankiewicz, Herman Mankiewicz's widow, who was
traveling for six months, and although she had packed

away the china she did not want used along with Herman Mankiewicz's Academy Award for *Citizen Kane* (you'll have friends over, she had said, they'll get drunk, they'll want to play with it) she had left out her Minton dinner plates, the same pattern as the Minton tiles that line the arcade south of Bethesda Fountain in Central Park, for me to use. I had not used the Minton dinner plates before the christening but I put them on a buffet table that night for the fried chicken. I remember Diana eating a chicken wing off one of them, a fleck of rosemary from the chicken the only blemish on her otherwise immaculate manicure. The perfect baby slept in one of her two long white christening dresses (she had two long white christening dresses because she had been given two long white christening dresses, one batiste, the other linen, another homage) in the Saks bassinette. John's brother Nick took photographs. I look at those photographs now and am struck by how many of the women present were wearing Chanel suits and David Webb bracelets, and smoking cigarettes. It was a time of my life during which I actually believed that somewhere between frying the chicken to serve on Sara Mankiewicz's Minton dinner plates and buying the Porthault parasol to shade the beautiful baby girl in Saigon I had covered the main "motherhood" points.

15

There was a reason why I told you about Arcelia and the sixty dresses.

I was not unaware as I did so that a certain number of readers (more than some of you might think, fewer than the less charitable among you will think) would interpret this apparently casual information (she dressed her baby in clothes that needed washing and ironing, she had help in the house to do this washing and ironing) as evidence that Quintana did not have an "ordinary" childhood, that she was "privileged."

I wanted to lay this on the table.

"Ordinary" childhoods in Los Angeles very often involve someone speaking Spanish, but I will not make that argument.

Nor will I even argue that she had an "ordinary"

childhood, although I remain unsure about exactly who does.

"Privilege" is something else.

"Privilege" is a judgment.

"Privilege" is an opinion.

"Privilege" is an accusation.

"Privilege" remains an area to which—when I think of what she endured, when I consider what came later—I will not easily cop.

I look again at the photographs Nick took at the christening.

In fact the afternoon these photographs were taken, the afternoon at St. Martin of Tours and Sara Mankiewicz's house, the afternoon when Quintana wore the two christening dresses and I wore one of the pastel linen Donald Brooks dresses I had bought under the misunderstanding that they would be needed in Saigon, was never what I considered her "real" christening. (One question: would you have called buying pastel linen dresses for Saigon a mark of "privilege"? Or would you have called it more a mark of bone stupidity?) Her "real" christening had taken place in a tiled sink at the house in Portuguese Bend, a few days after we brought her home from the nursery at St. John's Hospital in Santa Monica. John had christened her himself, and told me only after the fact.

I recall a certain defensiveness on this issue.

What he said when he told me was not exactly along the lines of "I thought we might christen the baby, what do you think."

What he said when he told me was more along the lines of "I just christened the baby, take it or leave it."

It seemed that he had worried because the date I had arranged at St. Martin of Tours was two months away.

It seemed that he had not wanted to risk consigning our not yet christened baby to limbo.

I knew why he had not told me this before the fact.

He had not told me this before the fact because I was not a Catholic, and he had imagined objection.

Of the two of us, however, it was I who thought of that day in the tiled sink as the "real" christening.

The other christening, the christening at which the photographs were taken, was the "dress-up" christening.

Certain faces spring out at me from the photographs.

Connie Wald, wearing one of the several Chanel suits in evidence that afternoon, in her case one of blue-and-cream tweed lined in cyclamen-pink silk. It was Connie who gave Quintana one of the two long white dresses she wore at the church and after. Until Connie was in her nineties, when she developed a neuropathy, she still swam every day of her life. She cut back on the regimen of daily laps and stopped driving herself around Beverly Hills in an aged Rolls-Royce but otherwise continued exactly as before. She still wore the Claire McCardell dresses she had been given when she was a McCardell model in the 1940s. She still gave two or three dinner parties a week, cooked herself, mixed young and old in a way that flattered everyone present, lit huge fires in her library and filled the tables with salted almonds and fat pitchers of nasturtiums and the roses she still grew herself. Connie had been married to the producer Jerry Wald, who was said to have been Budd Schulberg's model for Sammy Glick in *What Makes Sammy Run* and who had died a few years before I met her. She once told me about the six weeks she spent in Nevada establishing the residency she needed to divorce her previous husband and marry Jerry Wald. She did not spend the six weeks in Las Vegas, because Las Vegas as we later knew it did not yet exactly exist. She spent the six weeks twenty miles from Las Vegas, in Boulder City, which had been built by the Bureau of Reclamation as the construction camp for Hoover Dam and in which both gambling and union membership were prohibited by law. I asked her what she had found to do for six weeks in Boulder City. She said that Jerry had given her a dog, which she walked, every day, through the identical streets lined with matching government bun-

galows that constituted Boulder City and on across the
dam. I recall this striking me as the most intrepid story
I ever heard about how someone did or did not stay in
Las Vegas, a topic not entirely deficient in intrepid
stories.

Diana.

Diana Lynn, Diana Hall.

Hers is another face that springs out from the photographs taken that day.

In this photograph she is holding a champagne flute
and smoking a cigarette. It occurs to me as I look at
her photograph that it was Diana who had made that
day possible. It was Diana who had drawn me into the
conversation about adoption over the New Year's
weekend on Morty's boat. It was Diana who had talked
to Blake Watson, it was Diana who had intuited how
deeply I needed Quintana. It was Diana who had
changed my life.

16

Some of us feel this overpowering need for a child and some of us don't. It had come over me quite suddenly, in my mid-twenties, when I was working for *Vogue*, a tidal surge. Once this surge hit I saw babies wherever I went. I followed their carriages on the street. I cut their pictures from magazines and tacked them on the wall next to my bed. I put myself to sleep by imagining them: imagining holding them, imagining the down on their heads, imagining the soft spots at their temples, imagining the way their eyes dilated when you looked at them.

Until then pregnancy had been only a fear, an accident to be avoided at any cost.

Until then I had felt nothing but relief at the moment each month when I started to bleed. If that moment was delayed by even a day I would leave my office at *Vogue* and, looking for instant reassurance

that I was not pregnant, go see my doctor, a Columbia
Presbyterian internist who had come to be known,
because his mother-in-law had been editor in chief of
Vogue and his office was always open to fretful staff
members, as "the *Vogue* doctor." I recall sitting in his
examining room on East Sixty-seventh Street one
morning waiting for the results of the most recent rabbit test I had implored him to do. He came into the
room whistling, and began misting the plants on the
window sill.

The test, I prompted.

He continued misting the plants.

I needed to know the results, I said, because I was
leaving to spend Christmas in California. I had the
ticket in my bag. I opened the bag. I showed him.

"You might not need a ticket to California," he said.
"You might need a ticket to Havana."

I correctly understood this to be intended as reas-
suring, his baroque way of saying that I might need an
abortion and that he could help me get one, yet my
immediate response was to vehemently reject the proposed solution: it was delusional, it was out of the
question, it was beyond discussion.

I couldn't possibly go to Havana.

There was a revolution in Havana.

In fact there was: it was December 1958, Fidel Cas-
tro would enter Havana within days.

I mentioned this.

"There's always a revolution in Havana," the *Vogue* doctor said.

A day later I started to bleed, and cried all night.

I thought I was regretting having missed this interesting moment in Havana but it turned out the surge had hit and what I was regretting was not having the baby, the still unmet baby, the baby I would eventually bring home from St. John's Hospital in Santa Monica. *What if you hadn't been home, what if you couldn't meet Dr. Watson at the hospital, what if there'd been an accident on the freeway, what would happen to me then.* Not long ago, when I read the fragment of the novel written just to show us, the scrap in which the protagonist thinks she might be pregnant and elects to address the situation by consulting her pediatrician, I remembered that morning on East Sixty-seventh Street. *Now, they didn't even care any more.*

17

There are certain moments in those first years with her that I remember very clearly.

These very clear moments stand out, recur, speak directly to me, on some levels flood me with pleasure and on others still break my heart.

I remember very clearly for example that her earliest transactions involved what she called "sundries." She invested this word, which she used as a synonym for "possessions" but seemed to derive from the "sundries shops" in the many hotels to which she had already been taken, with considerable importance, dizzying alternations of infancy and sophistication. One day after she had asked me for a Magic Marker I found her marking off an empty box into "drawers," or areas meant for specific of these "sundries." The "drawers" she designated were these: "Cash," "Passport," "My IRA," "Jewelry," and, finally—I find myself hardly able to tell you this—"Little Toys."

Again, the careful printing.

The printing alone I cannot forget.

The printing alone breaks my heart.

Another moment, not, on examination, dissimilar: I remember very clearly the Christmas night at her grandmother's house in West Hartford when John and I came in from a movie to find her huddled alone on the stairs to the second floor. The Christmas lights were off, her grandmother was asleep, everyone in the house was asleep, and she was patiently waiting for us to come home and address what she called "the new problem." We asked what the new problem was. "I just noticed I have cancer," she said, and pulled back her hair to show us what she had construed to be a growth on her scalp. In fact it was chicken pox, obviously contracted before she left nursery school in Malibu and just now surfacing, but had it been cancer, she had prepared her mind to be ready for cancer.

A question occurs to me:

Did she emphasize "new" when she mentioned "the new problem"?

Was she suggesting that there were also "old" problems, undetailed, problems with which she was for the moment opting not to burden us?

A third example: I remember very clearly the doll's house she constructed on the bookshelves of her bedroom at the beach. She had worked on it for several days, after studying a similar improvisation in an old copy of *House & Garden* ("Muffet Hemingway's doll's house" was how she identified the prototype, taking her cue from the *House & Garden* headline), but this was its first unveiling. Here was the living room, she explained, and here was the dining room, and here was the kitchen, and here was the bedroom.

I asked about an undecorated and apparently unallocated shelf.

That, she said, would be the projection room.

The projection room.

I tried to assimilate this.

Some people we knew in Los Angeles did in fact live in houses with projection rooms but to the best of my knowledge she had never seen one. These people who lived in houses with projection rooms belonged to our "working" life. She, I had imagined, belonged to our "private" life. Our "private" life, I had also imagined, was separate, sweet, inviolate.

I set this distinction to one side and asked how she planned to furnish the projection room.

There would need to be a table for the telephone to the projectionist, she said, then stopped to consider the empty shelf.

"And whatever I'll need for Dolby Sound," she added then.

As I describe these very clear memories I am struck by what they have in common: each involves her trying to handle adult life, trying to be a convincing grown-up person at an age when she was still entitled to be a small child. She could talk about "My IRA" and she could talk about "Dolby Sound" and she could talk about "just noticing" she had cancer, she could call Camarillo to find out what she needed to do if she was going crazy and she could call Twentieth Century–Fox to find out what she needed to do to be a star, but she was not actually prepared to act on whatever answers she got. "Little Toys" could still assume equal importance. She could still consult her pediatrician.

Was this confusion about where she stood in the chronological scheme of things our doing?

Did we demand that she be an adult?

Did we ask her to assume responsibility before she had any way of doing so?

Did our expectations prevent her from responding as a child?

I recall taking her, when she was four or five, up the coast to Oxnard to see *Nicholas and Alexandra*. On the drive home from Oxnard she referred to the czar and czarina as "Nicky and Sunny," and said, when asked how she had liked the picture, "I think it's going to be a big hit."

In other words, despite having just been told what had seemed to me as I watched it a truly harrowing story, a story that placed both parents and children in unthinkable peril—a peril to children more unthinkable still because its very source lay in the bad luck of having been born to these particular parents—she had resorted without hesitation to the local default response, which was an instant assessment of audience potential. Similarly, a few years later, taken to Oxnard to see *Jaws,* she had watched in horror, then, while I was still unloading the car in Malibu, skipped down to the beach and dove into the surf. About certain threats I considered real she remained in fact fearless. When she was eight or nine and enrolled in Junior Lifeguard, a program run by the Los Angeles County lifeguards that entailed being repeatedly taken out beyond the Zuma Beach breakers on a lifeguard boat and swimming back in, John and I arrived to pick her up and found the beach empty. Finally we saw her, alone, huddled in a towel behind a dune. The lifeguards, it seemed, were insisting, "for absolutely no reason," on taking everyone home. I said there must be a reason. "Only the sharks," she said. I looked at her. She was clearly disappointed, even a little disgusted, impatient with the turn the morning had taken. She shrugged. "They were just blues," she said then.

When I remember the "sundries" I am forced to remember the hotels in which she had stayed before she was five or six or seven. I say "forced to remember" because my images of her in these hotels are tricky. On the one hand those images survive as my truest memories of the paradox she was—of the child trying not to appear as a child, of the strenuousness with which she tried to present the face of a convincing adult. On the other hand it is just such images— the same images—that encourage a view of her as "privileged," somehow deprived of a "normal" childhood.

On the face of it she had no business in these hotels.

The Lancaster and the Ritz and the Plaza Athénée in Paris.

The Dorchester in London.

The St. Regis and the Regency in New York, and also the Chelsea. The Chelsea was for those trips to New York when we were not on expenses. At the Chelsea they would find her a crib downstairs and

John would bring her breakfast from the White Tower across the street.

The Fairmont and the Mark Hopkins in San Francisco.

The Kahala and the Royal Hawaiian in Honolulu. "Where did the morning went," she would ask at the Royal Hawaiian when she woke, still on mainland time, and found the horizon dark. "Imagine a five-year-old walking to the reef," she would say at the Royal Hawaiian, near a swoon, when we held her hands and swung her through the shallow sea.

The Ambassador and the Drake in Chicago.

It was at the Ambassador, in the Pump Room at midnight, that she ate caviar for the first time, a mixed success since she wanted it again at every meal thereafter and did not yet entirely understand the difference between "on expenses" and "not on expenses." She had happened to be in the Pump Room at midnight because we had taken her that night to Chicago Stadium to see a band we were following, Chicago, research for *A Star Is Born*. She had sat through the concert onstage, on one of the amps. The band had played "Does Anybody Really Know What Time It Is," and "25 or 6 to 4." She had referred to the band as "the boys."

When we left Chicago Stadium with the boys that night the crowd had rocked the car, delighting her.

She did not want to go to her grandmother's in West Hartford the next day, she had advised me when we got back to the Ambassador, she wanted to go to Detroit with the boys.

So much for keeping our "private" life separate from our "working" life.

In fact she was inseparable from our working life. Our working life was the very reason she happened to be in these hotels. When she was five or six, for example, we took her with us to Tucson, where *The Life and Times of Judge Roy Bean* was shooting. The Hilton Inn, where the production was based during its Tucson location, sent a babysitter to stay with her while we watched the dailies. The babysitter asked her to get Paul Newman's autograph. A crippled son was mentioned. Quintana got the autograph, delivered it to the babysitter, then burst into tears. It was never clear to me whether she was crying about the crippled son or about feeling played by the babysitter. Dick Moore was the cinematographer on *The Life and Times of Judge Roy Bean* but she seemed to make no connection between this Dick Moore she encountered at the Hilton Inn in Tucson and the Dick Moore she encountered on our beach. On our beach everyone was home, and so was she. At the Hilton Inn in Tucson everyone was working, and so was she. "Working" was a way of being she understood at her core. When she was nine I took her with me on an eight-city book tour: New York, Boston, Washington, Dallas, Houston, Los Angeles, San Francisco, Chicago. "How do you like our monuments," Katharine Graham had asked her in Washington. She had seemed mystified but game. "What monuments," she had asked with interest, entirely unaware that most children who visited Washington were shown the Lincoln Memorial instead of National Public Radio and *The Washington Post*. Her favorite city on this tour had been Dallas. Her least favorite had been Boston. Boston, she had complained, was "all white."

"You mean you didn't see many black people in Boston," Susan Traylor's mother had suggested when Quintana got back to Malibu and reported on her trip.

"No," Quintana said, definite on this point. "I mean it's not in color."

She had learned to order triple lamb chops from room service on this trip.

She had learned to sign her room number for Shirley Temples on this trip.

If a car or an interviewer failed to show up at the appointed time on this trip she had known what to do: check the schedule and "call Wendy," Wendy being the publicity director at Simon & Schuster. She knew which bookstores reported to which best-seller lists and she knew the names of their major buyers and she knew what a green room was and she knew what agents did. She knew what agents did because before she was four, on a day when my schedule for household help had fallen apart, I had taken her with me to a meeting at the William Morris office in Beverly Hills. I had prepared her, explained that the meeting was about earning the money that paid for the triple lamb chops from room service, impressed on her the need for not interrupting or asking when we could leave. This preparation, it turned out, was entirely unnecessary. She was far too interested to interrupt. She accepted a glass of water when one was offered to her, managed the heavy Baccarat glass without dropping it, listened attentively but did not speak. Only at the end of the meeting did she ask the William Morris agent the question apparently absorbing her: "But when do you give her the money?"

When we noticed her confusions did we consider our own?

I still have the "Sundries" box in my closet, marked as she marked it.

18

I do not know many people who think they have suc-
ceeded as parents. Those who do tend to cite the
markers that indicate (their own) status in the world:
the Stanford degree, the Harvard MBA, the summer
with the white-shoe law firm. Those of us less inclined
to compliment ourselves on our parenting skills, in
other words most of us, recite rosaries of our failures,
our neglects, our derelictions and delinquencies. The
very definition of success as a parent has undergone a
telling transformation: we used to define success as
the ability to encourage the child to grow into inde-
pendent (which is to say into adult) life, to "raise" the
child, to let the child go. If a child wanted to try out his
or her new bicycle on the steepest hill in the neighborhood, there may have been a pro forma reminder that
the steepest hill in the neighborhood descended into a
four-way intersection, but such a reminder, because

independence was still seen as the desired end of the day, stopped short of nagging. If a child elected to indulge in activity that could end badly, such negative possibilities may have gotten mentioned once, but not twice.

It so happened that I was a child during World War Two, which meant that I grew up in circumstances in which even more stress than usual was placed on independence. My father was a finance officer in the Army Air Corps, and during the early years of the war my mother and brother and I followed him from Fort Lewis in Tacoma to Duke University in Durham to Peterson Field in Colorado Springs. This was not hardship but neither was it, given the overcrowding and dislocation that characterized life near American military facilities in 1942 and 1943, a sheltered childhood. In Tacoma we were lucky enough to rent what was called a guest house but was actually one large room with its own entrance. In Durham we again lived in one room, this one not large and not with its own entrance, in a house that belonged to a Baptist preacher and his family. This room in Durham came with "kitchen privileges," which amounted in practice to occasional use of the family's apple butter. In Colorado Springs we lived, for the first time, in an actual house, a four-room bungalow near a psychiatric hospital, but did not unpack: there was no point in unpack-

ing, my mother pointed out, since "orders"—a myste-
rious concept that I took on faith—could arrive any
day.

My brother and I were expected in each of these
venues to adapt, make do, both invent a life and simul-
taneously accept that any life we invented would be
summarily upended by the arrival of "orders." Who
gave the orders was never clear to me. In Colorado
Springs, where my father was stationed for longer than
he had been in either Tacoma or Durham, my brother
scouted the neighborhood, and made friends. I trolled
the grounds of the psychiatric hospital, recorded the
dialogue I overheard, and wrote "stories." I did not
at the time think this an unreasonable alternative to
staying in Sacramento and going to school (later it
occurred to me that if I had stayed in Sacramento and
gone to school I might have learned to subtract, a skill
that remains unmastered), but it would have made no
difference if I had. There was a war in progress. That
war did not revolve around or in any way hinge upon
the wishes of children. In return for tolerating these
home truths, children were allowed to invent their
own lives. The notion that they could be left to their
own devices—were in fact best left so—went unques-
tioned.

Once the war was over, and we were again home in
Sacramento, this laissez-faire approach continued. I

remember getting my learner's driving permit at age fifteen-and-a-half and interpreting it as a logical mandate to drive from Sacramento to Lake Tahoe after dinner, two or three hours up one of the switchbacked highways into the mountains and, if you just turned around and kept driving, which was all we did, since we already had whatever we wanted to drink in the car with us, two or three hours back. This disappearance into the heart of the Sierra Nevada on what amounted to an overnight DUI went without comment from my mother and father. I remember, above Sacramento at about the same age, getting sluiced into a diversion dam while rafting on the American River, then dragging the raft upstream and doing it again. This too went without comment.

All gone.

Virtually unimaginable now.

No time left on the schedule of "parenting" for tolerating such doubtful pastimes.

Instead, ourselves the beneficiaries of this kind of benign neglect, we now measure success as the extent to which we manage to keep our children monitored, tethered, tied to us. Judith Shapiro, when she was president of Barnard, was prompted to write an op-ed piece in *The New York Times* advising parents to show a little more trust in their children, stop trying to manage every aspect of their college life. She mentioned the father who had taken a year off from his job to supervise the preparation of his daughter's college applications. She mentioned the mother who had accompanied her daughter to a meeting with her dean to discuss a research project. She mentioned the mother who had demanded, on the grounds that it was she who paid the tuition bills, that her daughter's academic transcript be sent to her directly.

"You pay $35,000 a year, you want services," Tamar Lewin of *The New York Times* was told by the director of "the parents' office" at Northeastern in Boston, an office devoted to the tending of parents having become a virtually ubiquitous feature of campus administration. For a *Times* piece a few years ago on the narrowing of the generation gap on campus, Ms. Lewin spoke not only to the tenders of the parents but also to the students themselves, one of whom, at George Washington University, allowed that she used well over three thousand cellphone minutes a month talking to her family. She seemed to view this family as an employable academic resource. "I might call my dad and say, 'What's going on with the Kurds?' It's a lot easier than looking it up. He knows a lot. I would trust almost anything my dad says." Asked if she ever thought she might be too close to her parents, another

George Washington student had seemed only puzzled: "They're our parents," she had said. "They're supposed to help us. That's almost their job."

We increasingly justify such heightened involvement with our children as essential to their survival. We keep them on speed dial. We watch them on Skype. We track their movements. We expect every call to be answered, every changed plan reported. We fantasize unprecedented new dangers in their every unsupervised encounter. We mention terrorism, we share anxious admonitions: "It's different now." "It's not the way it was." "You can't let them do what we did."

Yet there were always dangers to children.

Ask anyone who was a child during the supposedly idyllic decade advertised to us at the time as the reward for World War Two. New cars. New appliances. Women in high-heeled pumps and ruffled aprons removing cookie sheets from ovens enameled in post-war "harvest" colors: avocado, gold, mustard, brown, burnt orange. This was as safe as it got, except it wasn't: ask any child who was exposed during this postwar harvest fantasy to the photographs from Hiroshima and Nagasaki, ask any child who saw the photographs from the death camps.

"I *have to know* about this."

So Quintana said when I found her hiding under the

covers of her bed in Malibu, stunned, disbelieving, flashlight in hand, studying a book of old *Life* photographs that she had come across somewhere.

There were blue-and-white checked gingham curtains in the windows of her room in Malibu.

I remember them blowing as she showed me the book.

She was showing me the photographs Margaret Bourke-White did for *Life* of the ovens at Buchenwald.

That was what she *had to know.*

Or ask the child who would not allow herself to fall asleep during most of 1946 because she feared the fate of six-year-old Suzanne Degnan, who on January seventh of that year had been kidnapped from her bed in Chicago, dissected in a sink, and disposed of in pieces in the sewers of the far north side. Six months after Suzanne Degnan's disappearance a seventeen-year-old University of Chicago sophomore named William Heirens was arrested and sentenced to life imprisonment.

Or ask the child who nine years later followed the California search for fourteen-year-old Stephanie Bryan, who vanished while walking home from her Berkeley junior high school through the parking lot of the Claremont Hotel, her customary shortcut, and was next seen several hundred miles from Berkeley, buried in a shallow grave in California's most northern

mountains. Five months after Stephanie Bryan's disappearance a twenty-seven-year-old University of
California accounting student was arrested, charged
with her death, and within two years convicted and
executed in the gas chamber at San Quentin.

Since the events surrounding the disappearances
and deaths of both Suzanne Degnan and Stephanie
Bryan occurred in circulation areas served by aggres-
sive Hearst papers, both cases were extensively and
luridly covered. The lesson taught by the coverage was
clear: childhood is by definition perilous. To be a child
is to be small, weak, inexperienced, the dead bottom
of the food chain. Every child knows this, or did.

Knowing this is why children call Camarillo.

Knowing this is why children call Twentieth
Century–Fox.

"This case has been a haunting one all my life as I
was a grown-up eight-year-old when it happened and
followed it every day in the *Oakland Tribune* from day
one till the end." So wrote an internet correspondent
in response to a recent look back at the Stephanie
Bryan case. "I had to read it when my parents weren't
around as they didn't think it was fitting to be reading
about a homicide at my age."

As adults we lose memory of the gravity and terrors
of childhood.

Hello, Quintana. I'm going to lock you here in the garage.

After I became five I never ever dreamed about him.

I have to know about this.

One of her abiding fears, I learned much later, was that John would die and there would be no one but her to take care of me.

How could she have even imagined that I would not take care of her?

I used to ask that.

Now I ask the reverse:

How could she have even imagined that I *could* take care of her?

She saw me as needing care myself.

She saw me as frail.

Was that her anxiety or mine?

I learned about this fear when she was temporarily off the ventilator in one or another ICU, I have no memory which.

I told you, they were all the same.

The blue-and-white printed curtains. The gurgling through plastic tubing. The dripping from the IV line, the rales, the alarms.

The codes. The crash cart.

This was never supposed to happen to her.

It must have been the ICU at UCLA.

Only at UCLA was she off the ventilator long enough to have had this conversation.

You have your wonderful memories.

I do, but they blur.

They fade into one another.

They become, as Quintana a month or two later described the only memory she could summon of the five weeks she spent in the ICU at UCLA, "all mudgy."

I tried to tell her: I too have trouble remembering.

Languages mingle: do I need an *abogado* or do I need an *avocat?*

Names vanish. The names for example of California counties, once so familiar that I recited them in alphabetized order (Alameda and Alpine and Amador, Calaveras and Colusa and Contra Costa, Madera and Marin and Mariposa) now elude me.

The name of one county I do remember.

The name of this single county I always remember.

I had my own Broken Man.

I had my own stories about which I had to know.

Trinity.

The name of the county in which Stephanie Bryan had been found buried in the shallow grave was Trinity.

The name of the test site at Alamogordo that had led to the photographs from Hiroshima and Nagasaki was also Trinity.

19

"What we need here is a montage, music over.
How she: talked to her father and xxxx and
xxxxx—

"xx," he said.

"xxx," she said.

"How she:

"How she did this and *why* she did that and *what
the music was* when they did x and x and xxx—

"How he, and also she—"

The above are notes I made in 1995 for a novel I
published in 1996, *The Last Thing He Wanted.* I offer
them as a representation of how comfortable I used
to be when I wrote, how easily I did it, how little

thought I gave to what I was saying until I had already said it. In fact, in any real sense, what I was doing then was never writing at all: I was doing no more than sketching in a rhythm and letting that rhythm tell me what it was I was saying. Many of the marks I set down on the page were no more than "xxx," or "xxxx," symbols that meant "copy tk," or "copy to come," but do notice: such symbols were arranged in specific groupings. A single "x" differed from a double "xx," "xxx" from "xxxx." The number of such symbols had a meaning. The arrangement was the meaning.

The same passage, rewritten, which is to say "written" in any real sense at all, became more detailed: "What we want here is a montage, music over. *Angle on Elena.* Alone on the dock where her father berthed the *Kitty Rex.* Working loose a splinter on the planking with the toe of her sandal. Taking off her scarf and shaking out her hair, damp from the sweet heavy air of South Florida. *Cut to Barry Sedlow.* Standing in the door of the frame shack, under the sign that read RENTALS GAS BAIT BEER AMMO. Leaning against the counter. Watching Elena through the screen door as he waited for change. *Angle on the manager.* Sliding a thousand-dollar bill beneath the tray in the cash register, replacing the tray, counting out the hundreds. No place you could not pass a hundred. There in the sweet heavy air of South Florida. Havana so close you could see the two-tone Impalas on the Malecón. Goddamn but we had some fun there."

More detailed, yes.

"She" now has a name: Elena.

"He" now has a name: Barry Sedlow.

But again, do notice: it had all been there in the original notes. It had all been there in the symbols, the marks on the page. It had all been there in the "xxx" and the "xxxx."

I supposed this process to be like writing music.

I have no idea whether or not this was an accurate assessment, since I neither wrote nor read music. All I know now is that I no longer write this way. All I know now is that writing, or whatever it was I was doing when I could proceed on no more than "xxx" and "xxxx," whatever it was I was doing when I imagined myself hearing the music, no longer comes easily to me. For a while I laid this to a certain weariness with my own style, an impatience, a wish to be more direct. I encouraged the very difficulty I was having laying words on the page. I saw it as evidence of a new directness. I see it differently now. I see it now as frailty. I see it now as the very frailty Quintana feared.

We are moving into another summer.

I find myself increasingly focused on this issue of frailty.

I fear falling on the street, I imagine bicycle messengers knocking me to the ground. The approach of a child on a motorized scooter causes me to freeze mid-intersection, play dead. I no longer go for breakfast to Three Guys on Madison Avenue: what if I were to fall on the way?

I feel unsteady, unbalanced, as if my nerves are misfiring, which may or may not be an exact description of what my nerves are in fact doing.

I hear a new tone when acquaintances ask how I am, a tone I have not before noticed and find increasingly distressing, even humiliating: these acquaintances seem as they ask impatient, half concerned, half querulous, as if no longer interested in the answer.

As if all too aware that the answer will be a complaint.

I determine to speak, if asked how I am, only positively.

I frame the cheerful response.

What I believe to be the cheerful response as I frame it emerges, as I hear it, more in the nature of a whine.

Do not whine, I write on an index card. *Do not complain. Work harder. Spend more time alone.*

I push-pin the index card to the corkboard on which I collect notes.

"Struck by a train nine days before our wedding," one note on the corkboard reads. *"Left the house that morning and was killed that afternoon in the crash of a small plane,"* another reads. *"It was the second of January, 1931,"* a third reads. *"I ran a little coup. My brother became president. He was more mature. I went to Europe."*

These notes I push-pin to the corkboard are intended at the time I make them to restore my ability to function, but have so far not done so. I study the notes again. *Who* was struck by the train nine days before her wedding? Or was it nine days before *his* wedding? *Who* left the house that morning and was killed that afternoon in the crash of the small plane? *Who,* above all, ran the little coup on the second of January, 1931? And in what country?

I abandon the attempt to answer these questions.

The telephone rings.

Grateful for the interruption, I pick it up. I hear the voice of my nephew Griffin. He feels the need to report that he has been getting calls from "concerned friends." The focus of their concern is my health, specifically my weight. I am no longer grateful. I point out that I have weighed the same amount since the early 1970s, when I picked up paratyphoid during a film festival on the Caribbean coast of Colombia and by the time I got home had dropped so much weight that my mother had to fly to Malibu to feed me. Griffin says that he recognizes this. He is aware that my weight has not fluctuated since he was old enough to notice it. He is reporting only what these "concerned friends" have mentioned to him.

Griffin and I understand each other, which means in this case that we are able to change the subject. I consider asking him if he knows who it was who ran the little coup on the second of January, 1931, and in what country, but do not. In the absence of another subject I tell him about a taxi driver I recently encountered on my way from the Four Seasons Hotel in San Francisco to SFO. This taxi driver told me that he had been analyzing drill sites around Houston until the oil boom went belly up. His father had been a construction supervisor, he said, which meant that he had grown up on the construction sites of the big postwar high dams and power reactors. He mentioned Glen Canyon on the Colorado. He mentioned Rancho Seco outside Sacramento. He mentioned, when he learned that I was a writer, wanting himself to write a book about "intercourse between the United States and Japan." He had proposed such a book to Simon & Schuster but Simon & Schuster, he now believed, had passed the proposal on to another writer.

"Fellow by the name of Michael Crichton," he said. "I'm not saying he stole it, I'm just saying they used my ideas. But hey. Ideas are free."

Around San Bruno he began mentioning Scientology.

I tell you this true story just to prove that I can.

That my frailty has not yet reached a point at which I can no longer tell a true story.

Weeks pass, then months.

I go to a rehearsal room on West Forty-second Street to watch a run-through of a play, a new production of a Broadway musical for which two close friends wrote the lyrics in the 1970s.

I sit on a folding metal chair. Behind me I hear voices I recognize (the two close friends and their collaborator, who wrote the book) but I feel too uncertain to turn around. The songs, some familiar and some new, continue. The reprises roll around. As I sit on the folding metal chair I begin to fear getting up. As the finale approaches, I experience outright panic. What if my feet no longer move? What if my muscles lock? What if this neuritis or neuropathy or neurological inflammation has evolved into a condition more malign? I once in my late twenties had an exclusionary diagnosis of multiple sclerosis, believed later by the neurologist who made the diagnosis to be in remission, but what if it is no longer in remission? What if it never was? What if it has returned? What if I stand up from this folding chair in this rehearsal room on West Forty-second Street and collapse, fall to the floor, the folding metal chair collapsing with me?

Or what if—

(Another series of dire possibilities occurs to me, this series even more alarming than the last—)

What if the damage extends beyond the physical?

What if the problem is now cognitive?

What if the absence of style that I welcomed at one point—the directness that I encouraged, even cultivated—what if this absence of style has now taken on a pernicious life of its own?

What if my new inability to summon the right word,

the apt thought, the connection that enables the words to make sense, the rhythm, the music itself—

What if this new inability is systemic?

What if I can never again locate the words that work?

20

I see a new neurologist, at Columbia Presbyterian.

The new neurologist has answers: all new neurologists have answers, usually wishful. New neurologists remain the last true believers in the power of wishful thinking. The answers offered by this particular new neurologist are for me to gain weight and devote a minimum of three hours a week to physical therapy.

I have been through this catechism before.

I happen to have been a remarkably small child. I say remarkably for a reason: something about my size was such that perfect strangers could always be relied upon to remark on it. "You're not very thick," I recall a French doctor saying when I went to see him in Paris for an antibiotic prescription. This was true enough, but I grew tired of hearing it. I grew particularly tired of hearing it when it was presented as something I might otherwise have missed. I was short, I was thin, I could circle my wrists with my thumb and index finger. My earliest memories involve being urged by my mother to gain weight, as if my failure to do so were willful, an act of rebellion. I was not allowed to get up from the table until I had eaten everything on my plate, a rule that led mainly to new and inventive ways of eating nothing on my plate. The "clean-plate club" was frequently mentioned. "Good eaters" were commended. "She's not a human garbage can," I recall my father exploding in my defense. As an adult I came to see this approach to food as more or less guaranteeing an eating disorder, but I never mentioned this theory to my mother.

Nor do I mention it to the new neurologist.

Actually the new neurologist offers, in addition to gaining weight and doing physical therapy, a third, although equally wishful, answer: the exclusionary diagnosis I received in my late twenties notwithstanding, I do not have multiple sclerosis. He is vehement on this point. There is no reason to believe that I have multiple sclerosis. Magnetic Resonance Imaging, a technique not yet available when I was in my late twenties, conclusively demonstrates that I do not have multiple sclerosis.

In that case, I ask, trying to summon an appearance of faith in whatever he chooses to answer, what is it that I do have?

I have neuritis, a neuropathy, a neurological inflammation.

I overlook the shrug.

I ask what caused this neuritis, this neuropathy, this neurological inflammation.

Not weighing enough, he answers.

It does not escape me that the consensus on what is wrong with me has once again insinuated the ball into my court.

I am referred to a dietitian on this matter of gaining weight.

The dietitian makes (the inevitable) protein shakes, brings me freshly laid eggs (better) from a farm in New Jersey and perfect vanilla ice cream (better still) from Maison du Chocolat on Madison Avenue.

I drink the protein shakes.

I eat the freshly laid eggs from the farm in New Jersey and the perfect vanilla ice cream from Maison du Chocolat on Madison Avenue.

Nonetheless.

I do not gain weight.

I have an uneasy sense that the consensus solution has already failed.

I find, on the other hand, somewhat to my surprise, that I actively like physical therapy. I keep regular appointments at a Columbia Presbyterian sports medicine facility at Sixtieth and Madison. I am impressed

by the strength and general tone of the other patients
who turn up during the same hour. I study their balance, their proficiency with the various devices recommended by the therapist. The more I watch, the
more encouraged I am: *this stuff really works,* I tell
myself. The thought makes me cheerful, optimistic. I
wonder how many appointments it will take to reach
the apparently effortless control already achieved by
my fellow patients. Only during my third week of
physical therapy do I learn that these particular fellow
patients are in fact the New York Yankees, loosening
up between game days.

21

Today as I walk home from the Columbia Presbyterian sports medicine facility at Sixtieth and Madison I find the optimism engendered by proximity to the New York Yankees fading. In fact my physical confidence seems to be reaching a new ebb. My cognitive confidence seems to have vanished altogether. Even the correct stance for telling you this, the ways to describe what is happening to me, the attitude, the tone, the very words, now elude my grasp.

The tone needs to be direct.

I need to talk to you directly, I need to *address the subject as it were*, but something stops me.

Is this another kind of neuropathy, a new frailty, am I no longer able to talk directly?

Was I ever?

Did I lose it?

Or is the subject in this case a matter I wish not to address?

When I tell you that I am afraid to get up from a folding chair in a rehearsal room on West Forty-second Street, of what am I really afraid?

22

What if you hadn't been home when Dr. Watson
      called—
What if you couldn't meet him at the hospital—
What if there'd been an accident on the freeway—
What would happen to me then?

All adopted children, I am told, fear that they will be abandoned by their adoptive parents as they believe themselves to have been abandoned by their natural. They are programmed, by the unique circumstances of their introduction into the family structure, to see abandonment as their role, their fate, the destiny that will overtake them unless they outrun it.

Quintana.

All adoptive parents, I do not need to be told, fear that they do not deserve the child they were given, that the child will be taken from them.

Quintana.

Quintana is one of the areas about which I have difficulty being direct.

I said early on that adoption is hard to get right but I did not tell you why.

"Of course you won't tell her she's adopted," many people said at the time she was born, most of these people the age of my parents, a generation, like that of Diana's parents, for which adoption remained obscurely shameful, a secret to be kept at any cost. "You couldn't possibly tell her."

Of course we could possibly tell her.

In fact we had already told her. *L'adoptada, m'ija.* There was never any question of not telling her. What were the alternatives? Lie to her? Leave it to her agent to take her to lunch at the Beverly Hills Hotel? Before too many years passed I would write about her adoption, John would write about her adoption, Quintana herself would agree to be one of the children interviewed for a book by the photographer Jill Krementz called *How It Feels to Be Adopted.* Over those years we had received periodic communications from women who had seen these mentions of her adoption and believed her to be their own lost daughter, women who had themselves given up infants for adoption and were now haunted by the possibility that this child about whom they had read could be that missing child.

This beautiful child, this perfect child.

Qué hermosa, qué chula.

We responded to each of these communications, we followed up, we explained how the facts did not coincide, the dates did not tally, why the perfect child could not be theirs.

We considered our role fulfilled, the case closed.

Still.

The recommended choice narrative did not end, as I had imagined it would (hoped it would, dreamed it would), with the perfect child placed on the table between us for lunch at The Bistro (Sidney Korshak's corner banquette, the blue-and-white dotted organdy dress) on the hot day in September 1966 when the adoption became final.

Thirty-two years later, in 1998, on a Saturday morning when she was alone in her apartment and vulnerable to whatever bad or good news arrived at her door, the perfect child received a Federal Express letter from a young woman who convincingly identified herself as her sister, her full sister, one of two younger children later born, although we had not before known this, to Quintana's natural mother and father. At the time of Quintana's birth the natural mother and father had not yet been married. At a point after her birth they married, had the two further children, Quintana's full sister and brother, and then divorced. According to the letter from the young woman who identified herself as Quintana's sister, the mother and sister lived now in Dallas. The brother, from whom the mother was estranged, lived in another city in Texas. The father, who had remarried and fathered another child, lived in Florida. The sister, who had learned from her mother only a few weeks before that Quintana existed, had determined immediately, against the initial instincts of her mother, to locate her.

She had resorted to the internet.

On the internet she had found a private detective who said that he could locate Quintana for two hundred dollars.

Quintana had an unlisted telephone number.

The two hundred dollars was for accessing her Con Ed account.

The sister had agreed to the deal.

It had taken the detective only ten further minutes to call the sister back with a street address and apartment number in New York.

14 Sutton Place South. Apartment 11D.

The sister had written the letter.

She had sent it to Apartment 11D at 14 Sutton Place South via Federal Express.

"Saturday delivery," Quintana said when she showed us the letter, still in its Federal Express envelope. "The FedEx came *Saturday delivery*." I remember her repeating these words, emphasizing them, *Saturday delivery, the FedEx came Saturday delivery,* as if maintaining focus on this one point could put her world back together.

23

I cannot easily express what I thought about this.

On the one hand, I told myself, it could hardly be a surprise. We had spent thirty-two years considering just such a possibility. We had for many of those years seen such a possibility even as a probability. Quintana's mother, through a bureaucratic error on the part of the social worker, had been told not only our names and Quintana's name but the name under which I wrote. We did not lead an entirely private life. We gave lectures, we attended events, we got photographed. We could be easily found. We had discussed how it would happen. There would be a letter. There would be a phone call. The caller would say such and such. Whichever one of us took the call would say such and such and such. We would meet.

It would be logical.

It would all, when it happened, make sense.

In an alternate scenario, Quintana herself would choose to undertake the search, initiate the contact. Should she wish to do so, the process would be simple. Through another bureaucratic error, a bill from St. John's Hospital in Santa Monica had reached us without the mother's name redacted. I had seen the name only once but it had remained imprinted on my memory. I had thought it a beautiful name.

We had discussed this with our lawyer. We had authorized him, should Quintana ask, to give her whatever help she wanted or needed.

This too would be logical.

This too would all, when it happened, make sense.

On the other hand, I told myself, it now seemed too late, not the right time.

There comes a point, I told myself, at which a family is, for better or for worse, finished.

Yes. I just told you. *Of course* I had considered this possibility.

Accepting it would be something else.

A while back, to another point, I mentioned that we had taken her with us to Tucson while *The Life and Times of Judge Roy Bean* was shooting there.

I mentioned the Hilton Inn and I mentioned the babysitter and I mentioned Dick Moore and I mentioned Paul Newman but there was a part of that trip that I did not mention.

It happened on our first night in Tucson.

We had left her with the babysitter. We had watched the dailies. We had met in the Hilton Inn dining room for dinner. Halfway through dinner—a few too many people at the table, a little too much noise, just another working dinner on a motion picture on just another location—it had struck me: this was not, for me, just another location.

This was Tucson.

We had not been told much about her natural family but we had been told one thing: her mother was from Tucson. Her mother was from Tucson and I knew her mother's name.

I never considered not doing what I did next.

I got up from dinner and found a pay phone with a Tucson telephone book.

I looked up the name.

I showed the name to John.

Without discussion we went back to the crowded table in the dining room and told the producer of *The Life and Times of Judge Roy Bean* that we needed to speak to him. He followed us into the lobby. There in a corner of the lobby of the Hilton Inn we talked to him for three or four minutes. It was imperative, we said, that no one should know we were in Tucson. It was especially imperative, we said, that no one should know Quintana was in Tucson. I did not want to pick up the Tucson paper, I said, and see any cute items about children on the *Judge Roy Bean* location. I asked him to alert the unit publicity people. I stressed that under no condition should Quintana's name appear in connection with the picture.

There was no reason to think that it would but I had to be sure.

I had to cover that base.

I had to make that effort.

I believed as I did so that I was protecting both Quintana and her mother.

I tell you this now by way of suggesting the muddled impulses that can go hand in hand with adoption.

A few months after the arrival of the FedEx Saturday delivery, Quintana and her sister met, first in New York and then in Dallas. In New York Quintana showed her visiting sister Chinatown. She took her shopping at Pearl River. She brought her to dinner

with John and me at Da Silvano. She invited her
friends and cousins to her apartment for drinks so that
they and her sister could all meet. The two sisters
looked like twins. When Griffin walked into Quintana's apartment and saw the sister he inadvertently
greeted her as "Q." Margaritas were mixed. Gua-
camole was made. There was about this initial weekend meeting a spirit of willed excitement, determined
camaraderie, resolute discovery.

It would be a month or so later, in Dallas, before the
will and the determination and the resolution all failed
her.

When she called after twenty-four hours in Dallas
she had seemed distraught, on the edge of tears.

In Dallas she had been introduced for the first time
not only to her mother but to many other members
of what she was now calling her "biological family,"
strangers who welcomed her as their long-missing
child.

In Dallas these strangers had shown her snapshots,
remarked on her resemblance to one or another cousin
or aunt or grandparent, seemingly taken for granted
that she had chosen by her presence to be one of them.

On her return to New York she had begun getting
regular calls from her mother, whose initial resistance
to the idea of a reunion (in the first place it wasn't a

reunion, her mother had punctiliously pointed out, since they had never met in the first place) seemed to have given way to a need to discuss the events that had led to the adoption. These calls came in the morning, typically at a time when Quintana was just about to leave for work. She did not want to cut her mother short but neither did she want to be late for work, particularly because *Elle Décor*, the magazine for which she was at that time the photography editor, was undergoing a staff realignment and she felt her job to be in jeopardy. She discussed this conflict with a psychiatrist. After the discussion with the psychiatrist she wrote to her mother and sister saying that "being found" ("I was found" had evolved into her arrestingly equivocal way of referring to what had happened) was proving "too much to handle," "too much and too soon," that she needed to "step back," "catch up for a while" with what she still considered her real life.

In reply she received a letter from her mother saying that she did not want to be a burden and so had disconnected her telephone.

This was the point at which it seemed clear that not one of us would escape those muddled impulses.

Not Quintana's mother, not Quintana's sister, certainly not me.

Not even Quintana.

Quintana who referred to the shattering of her known world as "being found."

Quintana who had called Nicholas and Alexandra "Nicky and Sunny" and seen their story as "a big hit."

Quintana who had imagined The Broken Man in such convincing detail.

Quintana who told me that after she became five she never ever dreamed about The Broken Man.

A few weeks after her mother disconnected her telephone another message arrived, although not from her mother and not from her sister.

She received a letter from her natural father in Florida.

Over the time that passed between the time she knew herself to have been adopted and the time she was "found," a period of some thirty years, she had many times mentioned her other mother. "My other mommy," and later "my other mother," had been from the time she first spoke the way she referred to her. She had wondered who and where this other mother was. She had wondered what she looked like. She had considered and ultimately rejected the possibility of finding out. John had once asked her, when she was small, what she would do if she met her "other mommy." "I'd put one arm around Mom," she had said, "and one arm around my other mommy, and I'd say 'Hello, Mommies.' "

She had never, not once, mentioned her other father.

I have no idea why but the picture in her mind seemed not to include a father.

"What a long strange journey this has been," the letter from Florida read.

She burst into tears as she read it to me.

"On top of everything else," she said through the tears, "my father has to be a Deadhead."

Three years later the final message arrived, this one from her sister.

Her sister wanted her to know that their brother had died. The cause of death was unclear. His heart was mentioned.

Quintana had never met him.

I am not sure of the dates but I think he would have been born the year she was five.

After I became five I never ever dreamed about him.

This call to say that he had died may have been the last time the sisters spoke.

When Quintana herself died, her sister sent flowers.

24

I find myself leafing today for the first time through a journal she kept in the spring of 1984, a daily assignment for an English class during her senior year at the Westlake School for Girls. "I had an exciting revelation while studying a poem by John Keats," this volume of the journal begins, on a page dated March 7, 1984, the one-hundred-and-seventeenth entry since she had begun keeping the journal in September of 1983. "In the poem, 'Endymion,' there is a line that seems to tell my present fear of life: *Pass into nothingness.*"

This March 7, 1984, entry continues, moves into a discussion of Jean-Paul Sartre and Martin Heidegger and their respective understandings of the abyss, but I am no longer following the argument: automatically, without thinking, appallingly, as if she were still at the

Westlake School and had asked me to take a look at her paper, I am editing it.

For example:

Delete commas setting off title "Endymion."

"Tell," as in "a line that seems to tell my present fear of life," is of course wrong.

"Describe" would be better.

"Suggest" would be better still.

On the other hand: "tell" might work: try "tell" as she uses it.

I try it: *She "tells" her present fear of life in relation to Sartre.*

I try it again: *She "tells" her present fear of life in relation to Heidegger. She "tells" her understanding of the abyss. She qualifies her understanding of the abyss: "This is merely how I interpret the abyss; I could be wrong."*

Considerable time passes before I realize that my preoccupation with the words she used has screened off any possible apprehension of what she was actually saying when she wrote her journal entry on that March day in 1984.

Was that deliberate?

Was I screening off what she said about her fear of life the same way I had screened off what she said about her fear of The Broken Man?

Hello, Quintana? I'm going to lock you here in the garage?

After I became five I never ever dreamed about him?

Did I all her life keep a baffle between us?

Did I prefer not to hear what she was actually saying?

Did it frighten me?

I try the passage again, this time reading for meaning.

What she said: *My present fear of life.*

What she said: *Pass into nothingness.*

What she was actually saying: *The World has nothing but Morning and Night. It has no Day or Lunch. Let me just be in the ground. Let me just be in the ground and go to sleep.* When I tell you that I am afraid to get up from a folding chair in a rehearsal room on West Forty-second Street, is this what I am actually saying?

Does it frighten me?

25

Let me again try to talk to you directly.

On my last birthday, December 5, 2009, I became seventy-five years old.

Notice the odd construction there—*I became seventy-five years old*—do you hear the echo?

I *became* seventy-five? I *became* five?

After I became five I never ever dreamed about him?

Also notice—in notes that talk about aging in their first few pages, notes called *Blue Nights* for a reason, notes called *Blue Nights* because at the time I began them I could think of little other than the inevitable approach of darker days—how long it took me to tell you that one salient fact, how long it took me to *address the subject as it were*. Aging and its evidence remain life's most predictable events, yet they also remain matters we prefer to leave unmentioned, unexplored: I have watched tears flood the eyes of grown women, loved women, women of talent and accomplishment, for no reason other than that a small child in the room, more often than not an adored niece or nephew, has just described them as "wrinkly," or asked how old they are. When we are asked this question we are always undone by its innocence, somehow shamed by the clear bell-like tones in which it is asked. What shames us is this: the answer we give is never innocent. The answer we give is unclear, evasive, even guilty. Right now when I answer this question I find myself doubting my own accuracy, rechecking the increasingly undoable arithmetic (born December 5 1934, subtract 1934 from 2009, do this in your head and watch yourself get muddled by the interruption of the entirely irrelevant millennium), insisting to myself (no one else particularly cares) that there must be a mistake: only yesterday I was in my fifties, my forties, only yesterday I was thirty-one.

Quintana was born when I was thirty-one.

Only yesterday Quintana was born.

Only yesterday I was taking Quintana home from the nursery at St. John's Hospital in Santa Monica.

Enveloped in a silk-lined cashmere wrapper.

Daddy's gone to get a rabbit skin to wrap his baby bunny in.

What if you hadn't been home when Dr. Watson called?

What would happen to me then?

Only yesterday I was holding her in my arms on the 405.

Only yesterday I was promising her that she would be safe with us.

We then called the 405 the San Diego Freeway.

It was only yesterday when we still called the 405 the San Diego, it was only yesterday when we still called the 10 the Santa Monica, it was only the day before yesterday when the Santa Monica did not yet exist.

Only yesterday I could still do arithmetic, remember telephone numbers, rent a car at the airport and drive it out of the lot without freezing, stopping at the key moment, feet already on the pedals but immobilized by the question of which is the accelerator and which the brake.

Only yesterday Quintana was alive.

I disengage my feet from the pedals, first one, then the other.

I invent a reason for the Hertz attendant to start the rental car.

I am seventy-five years old: this is not the reason I give.

26

A doctor to whom I occasionally talk suggests that I
have made an inadequate adjustment to aging.

Wrong, I want to say.

In fact I have made no adjustment whatsoever to
aging.

In fact I had lived my entire life to date without seriously believing that I would age.

I had no doubt that I would continue to wear the red
suede sandals with four-inch heels that I had always
preferred.

I had no doubt that I would continue to wear the
gold hoop earrings on which I had always relied, the
black cashmere leggings, the enameled beads.

My skin would develop flaws, fine lines, even brown
spots (this, at seventy-five, was what passed for a real-
istic cosmetic assessment), but it would continue to
look as it had always looked, basically healthy. My

hair would lose its original color but color could continue to be replaced by leaving the gray around the face and twice a year letting Johanna at Bumble and Bumble highlight the rest. I would recognize that the models I encountered on these semiannual visits to the color room at Bumble and Bumble were significantly younger than I was, but since these models I encountered on my semiannual visits to the color room at Bumble and Bumble were at most sixteen or seventeen there could be no reason to interpret the difference as a personal failure. My memory would slip but whose memory does not slip. My eyesight would be more problematic than it might have been before I began seeing the world through sudden clouds of what looked like black lace and was actually blood, the residue of a series of retinal tears and detachments, but there would still be no question that I could see, read, write, navigate intersections without fear.

No question that it could not be fixed.

Whatever "it" was.

I believed absolutely in my own power to surmount the situation.

Whatever "the situation" was.

When my grandmother was seventy-five she experienced a cerebral hemorrhage, fell unconscious to the sidewalk not far from her house in Sacramento, was taken to Sutter Hospital, and died there that night. This was "the situation" for my grandmother. When my mother was seventy-five she was diagnosed with breast cancer, did two cycles of chemotherapy, could not tolerate the third or fourth, nonetheless lived until she was two weeks short of her ninety-first birthday (when she did die it was of congestive heart failure, not cancer) but was never again exactly as she had been. Things went wrong. She lost confidence. She became apprehensive in crowds. She was no longer entirely comfortable at the weddings of her grandchildren or even, in truth, at family dinners. She made mystifying, even hostile, judgments. When she came to visit me in New York for example she pronounced St. James' Episcopal Church, the steeple and slate roof of which constitute the entire view from my living room windows, "the single ugliest church I have ever seen." When, on her own coast and at her own suggestion, I took her to see the jellyfish at the Monterey Bay Aquarium, she fled to the car, pleading vertigo from the movement of the water.

I recognize now that she was feeling frail.

I recognize now that she was feeling then as I feel now.

Invisible on the street.

The target of any wheeled vehicle on the scene.

Unbalanced at the instant of stepping off a curb, sitting down or standing up, opening or closing a taxi door.

Cognitively challenged not only by simple arithmetic but by straightforward news stories, announced changes in traffic flow, the memorization of a telephone number, the seating of a dinner party.

"Estrogen actually made me feel better," she said to me not long before she died, after several decades without it.

Well, yes. Estrogen had made her feel better.

This turns out to have been "the situation" for most of us.

And yet:

And still:

Despite all evidence:

Despite recognizing that my skin and my hair and even my cognition are all reliant on the estrogen I no longer have:

Despite recognizing that I will not again wear the red suede sandals with the four-inch heels and despite recognizing that the gold hoop earrings and the black cashmere leggings and the enameled beads no longer exactly apply:

Despite recognizing that for a woman my age even to note such details of appearance will be construed by many as a manifestation of misplaced vanity:

Despite all that:

Nonetheless:

That being seventy-five could present as a significantly altered situation, an altogether different "it,"
did not until recently occur to me.

27

Something happened to me early in the summer.
Something that altered my view of my own possibilities, shortened, as it were, the horizon.

I still have no idea what time it was when it happened, or why it was that it happened, or even in any
exact way what it was that happened. All I know is that
midway through June, after walking home with a
friend after an early dinner on Third Avenue in the
eighties, I found myself waking on the floor of my bedroom, left arm and forehead and both legs bleeding,
unable to get up. It seemed clear that I had fallen, but
I had no memory of falling, no memory whatsoever of
losing balance, trying to regain it, the usual preludes
to a fall. Certainly I had no memory of losing con-
sciousness. The diagnostic term for what had happened (I was to learn before the night ended) was
"syncope," fainting, but discussions of syncope, cen-

tering as they did on "pre-syncope symptoms" (palpi-
tations, light-headedness, dizziness, blurred or tunnel
vision), none of which I could identify, seemed not to
apply.

I had been alone in the apartment.

There were thirteen telephones in the apartment,
not one of which was at that moment within reach.

I remember lying on the floor and trying to visualize
the unreachable telephones, count them off room by
room.

I remember forgetting one room and counting off the
telephones a second and then a third time.

This was dangerously soothing.

I remember deciding in the absence of any prospect
of help to go back to sleep for a while, on the floor, the
blood pooling around me.

I remember pulling a quilt down from a wicker
chest, the only object I could reach, and folding it
under my head.

I remember nothing else until I woke a second time
and managed on this attempt to summon enough trac-
tion to pull myself up.

At which point I called a friend.

At which point he came over.

At which point, since I was still bleeding, we took a
taxi to the emergency room at Lenox Hill Hospital.

It was I who said Lenox Hill.

Let me repeat: it was I who said Lenox Hill.

Weeks later, this one fact was still troubling me as much as anything else about the entire sequence of events that night: *it was I who said Lenox Hill.* I got into a taxi in front of my apartment, which happens to be equidistant from two hospitals, Lenox Hill and New York Cornell, *and I said Lenox Hill.* Saying Lenox Hill instead of New York Cornell did not demonstrate a developed instinct for self-preservation. Saying Lenox Hill instead of New York Cornell demonstrated only that I was at that moment incapable of taking care of myself. Saying Lenox Hill instead of New York Cornell proved the point humiliatingly made by every nurse and aide and doctor to whom I spoke in the two nights I would eventually spend at Lenox Hill, the first night in the emergency room and the second in a cardiac unit, where a bed happened to be available and where it was erroneously assumed that because I had been given a bed in the cardiac unit I must have a cardiac problem: I was old. I was too old to live alone. I was too old to be allowed out of bed. I was too old even to recognize that if I had been given a bed in the cardiac unit I must have a cardiac problem.

"Your cardiac problem isn't showing up on the monitors," one nurse kept reporting, accusingly.

I tried to process what she was saying.

Processing what people were saying was not at that moment my long suit, but this nurse seemed to be suggesting that my "cardiac problem" was not showing up on the monitors because I had deliberately detached the electrodes.

I countered.

I said that to the best of my knowledge I did not have a cardiac problem.

She countered.

"Of course you have a cardiac problem," she said. And then, closing the issue: "Because otherwise you wouldn't be in the cardiac unit."

I had no answer for that.

I tried to pretend I was home.

I tried to figure out whether it was day or night: if it was day I had a shot at going home, but in the hospital there was no day or night.

Only shifts.

Only waiting.

Waiting for the IV nurse, waiting for the nurse with the narcotics key, waiting for the transporter.

Will someone please take the catheter out.

That transfusion was ordered at eleven this evening.

"How do you normally get around your apartment," someone in scrubs kept asking, marveling at what he seemed to consider my entirely unearned mobility, finally providing his own answer: "Walker?"

Demoralization occurs in the instant: I have trouble expressing the extent to which two nights of relatively undemanding hospitalization negatively affected me. There had been no surgery. There had been no uncomfortable procedures. There had been no real discomfort at all, other than emotional. Yet I felt myself to be the victim of a gross misunderstanding: I wanted only to go home, get the blood washed out of my hair, stop being treated as an invalid. Instead the very opposite was happening. My own doctor, who was based at Columbia Presbyterian, happened to be in St. Petersburg with his family: he called me at Lenox Hill during an intermission at the Kirov Ballet. He wanted to know what I was doing at Lenox Hill. So, at that point, did I. The doctors on the scene, determined to track down my phantom "cardiac problem," seemed willing to permanently infantilize me. Even my own friends, dropping by after work, very much in charge, no blood in their hair, sentient adults placing and receiving calls, making arrangements for dinner, bringing me perfect chilled soups that I could not eat because the hospital bed was so angled as to prevent sitting upright, were now talking about the need to get me "someone in the house": it was increasingly as if I had taken a taxi to Lenox Hill and woken up in *Driving Miss Daisy*.

With effort, I managed to convey this point.

I got released from Lenox Hill.

My own doctor got back from St. Petersburg.

After further days of unproductive cardiac monitoring the cardiac hypothesis was abandoned.

An appointment was made with yet another new neurologist, this one at NewYork Cornell.

Many tests were scheduled and done.

A new MRI, to establish whether or not there had been significant changes.

There had not been.

A new MRA, to see whether or not there had been any enlargement of the aneurysm visualized on the previous MRAs.

There had not been.

A new ultrasound, to establish whether or not there had been increased calcification of the carotid artery.

There had not been.

And, finally, a full-body PET scan, meant to show any abnormalities in the heart, the lungs, the liver, the kidneys, the bones, the brain: in fact anywhere in the body.

I repeatedly slid in and out of the PET scanner.

Forty minutes passed, then a change of position and another fifteen.

I lay motionless on the scanner.

It seemed impossible to imagine this coming up clean.

It would be one more version of the bed in the cardiac unit: a full-body PET scan had been ordered, *ergo,* as night follows day, there would need to be abnormalities for the full-body PET scan to show.

A day later I was given the results.

There were, surprisingly, no abnormalities seen in the scan.

Everyone agreed on this point. Everyone used the word "surprisingly."

Surprisingly, there were no abnormalities to explain why I felt as frail as I did.

Surprisingly, there were no abnormalities to tell me why I was afraid to get up from a folding chair in a rehearsal room on West Forty-second Street.

Only then did I realize that during the three weeks that had passed between taking the taxi to Lenox Hill, on the fourteenth of June, and receiving the results of the full-body PET scan, on the eighth of July, I had allowed this year's most deeply blue nights to come and go without my notice.

What does it cost to lose those weeks, that light, the very nights in the year preferred over all others?

Can you evade the dying of the brightness?

Or do you evade only its warning?

Where are you left if you miss the message the blue nights bring?

"Have you ever had a moment where everything in your life just stopped?" This was the way that this question was raised by Kris Jenkins, a three-hundred-and-sixty-pound Jets defensive tackle, after he tore, six plays into his tenth NFL season, both his meniscus and his anterior cruciate ligament. "So fast, but in slow motion? Like all your senses shut down? Like you're watching yourself?"

I offer you a second way of approaching the moment where everything in your life just stops, this one from the actor Robert Duvall: "I exist very nicely between the words 'action' and 'cut.'"

And even a third way: "It doesn't present as pain," I once heard an oncological surgeon say of cancer.

28

I find myself thinking exclusively about Quintana.
I need her with me.

Behind the house on Franklin Avenue in Hollywood in which we lived from the day we left Sara Mankiewicz's Minton plates until the day we moved into the beach house, a period of some four years, there was a clay tennis court, weeds growing through the cracked clay. I remember watching her weed it, kneeling on fat baby knees, the ragged stuffed animal she addressed as "Bunny Rabbit" at her side.

Daddy's gone to get a rabbit skin to wrap his baby bunny in.

In a few weeks she will have been dead five years.

Five years since the doctor said that the patient had been unable to get enough oxygen through the vent for at least an hour now.

Five years since Gerry and I left her in the ICU overlooking the river at New York Cornell.

I can now afford to think about her.

I no longer cry when I hear her name.

I no longer imagine the transporter being called to take her to the morgue after we left the ICU.

Yet I still need her with me.

In lieu of her presence I leaf through the books on a table in my office, each one a book she gave me.

One is called *Baby Animals and Their Mothers*, and is just that, black-and-white photographs of baby animals and their mothers: mostly comforting favorites (not unlike Bunny Rabbit), lambs and ewes, foals and mares, but also less common baby animals and their mothers: hedgehogs, koala bears, llamas. Stuck in the pages of *Baby Animals and Their Mothers* I find a French postcard showing a baby polar bear and its mother. *"Câlin sur la banquise,"* the caption reads in French, and then, in English: "Cuddling on the ice floe."

"Just a few things I found on my travels that reminded me of you," the note on the card reads, in printing less careful than it once was but still recognizable.

Still hers.

Beneath *Baby Animals and Their Mothers* is Jean-

Dominique Bauby's *The Diving Bell and the Butterfly*,
an account, by a former editor in chief of French *Elle*,
of what it had felt like to have a cerebrovascular accident on a date he knew to have been the eighth of
December and next wake at the end of January, unable
to speak, able to move only by blinking one eyelid: the
condition known as "locked-in syndrome." (Did anyone use the word "syncope"? Did anyone use the
words "pre-syncope symptoms"? Can we find any
clues here? Any clue to Jean-Dominique Bauby's situation? Any clue to my own?) For reasons that I did not
at the time entirely understand and have not since
wanted to explore, *The Diving Bell and the Butterfly*
had been when it was published extremely meaningful
to Quintana, so markedly so that I never told her that I
did not much like it, or for that matter even entirely
believe it.

Only later, when she was for most purposes locked
into her own condition, confined to a wheelchair and
afflicted by the detritus of a bleed into her brain and
the subsequent neurosurgery, did I begin to see its
point.

Beginning to see its point was when I stopped wanting to explore the reasons why it might have been so
markedly meaningful to Quintana.

Just let me be in the ground.

Just let me be in the ground and go to sleep.

I return *The Diving Bell and the Butterfly* to the table in my office.

I align it with *Baby Animals and Their Mothers*.

Colin sur la banquise.

This business of the ice floes is familiar to me. I did not need *Baby Animals and Their Mothers* to bring the image of the ice floes alive. In the first year of Quintana's hospitalizations I had watched ice floes from her hospital windows: ice floes on the East River from her windows at Beth Israel North, ice floes on the Hudson from her windows at Columbia Presbyterian. I think now of those ice floes and imagine having seen, floating past on one or another slab of breaking ice, a baby polar bear and its mother, heading for the Hell Gate Bridge.

I imagine having shown the baby polar bear and its mother to Quintana.

Colin sur la banquise.

Just let me be in the ground.

I resolve to forget the ice floes.

I have thought enough about the ice floes.

Thinking about the ice floes is like thinking about the transporter being called to take her to the morgue.

I walk into Central Park and sit for a while on a bench to which is attached a brass plaque indicating that a memorial contribution has been made to the Central Park Conservancy. There are now in the park many such brass plaques, many such benches. *"Quintana Roo Dunne Michael 1966–2005,"* the plaque on this bench reads. *"In summertime and wintertime."* A friend had made the contribution, and asked me to write out what I wanted the plaque to read. The same friend had come to visit Quintana when she was doing therapy in the neuro-rehab unit at UCLA, and after she saw Quintana had a cafeteria lunch with me in the hospital patio. It did not occur to either of us on the day we had the cafeteria lunch in the hospital patio at UCLA that Quintana's recovery would end at this bench.

So we still thought of that year.

Quintana's "recovery."

We had no idea then how rare recovery can be.

No idea that "recovery," like "adoption," remains one of those concepts that sounds more plausible than it turns out to be.

Colin sur la banquise.

The wheelchair.

The detritus of the bleed, the neurosurgery.

In summertime and wintertime.

I wonder if in those revised circumstances she remembered *The Diving Bell and the Butterfly,* what it meant to her then.

She did not want to talk about those revised circumstances.

She wanted to believe that if she did not "dwell" on them she would wake one morning and find them corrected.

"Like when someone dies," she once said by way of explaining her approach, "don't dwell on it."

29

Stop all the clocks, cut off the telephone,
Prevent the dog from barking with a juicy bone,
Silence the pianos and with muffled drum
Bring out the coffin, let the mourners come.

Let aeroplanes circle moaning overhead
Scribbling on the sky the message He Is Dead,
Put crêpe bows round the white necks of the public
  doves,
Let the traffic policemen wear black cotton gloves.

He was my North, my South, my East and West,
My working week and my Sunday rest,
My noon, my midnight, my talk, my song;
I thought that love would last for ever: I was
  wrong.

The stars are not wanted now; put out every one,
Pack up the moon and dismantle the sun,
Pour away the ocean and sweep up the wood;
For nothing now can ever come to any good.

So go W. H. Auden's "Funeral Blues," sixteen lines that, during the days and weeks immediately after John died, spoke directly to the anger—the unreasoning fury, the blind rage—that I found myself feeling. I later showed "Funeral Blues" to Quintana. I told her that I was thinking of reading it at the memorial service she and I were then planning for John. She implored me not to do so. She said she liked nothing about the poem. She said it was "wrong." She was vehement on this point. At the time I thought she was upset by the tone of the poem, its raw rhythms, the harshness with which it rejects the world, the sense it gives off of a speaker about to explode. I now think of her vehemence differently. I now think she saw "Funeral Blues" as dwelling on it.

On the afternoon she herself died, August 26, 2005, her husband and I left the ICU overlooking the river at

New York Cornell and walked through Central Park. The leaves on the trees were already losing their intensity, still weeks from dropping but ready to drop, not exactly faded but fading. At the time she entered the hospital, late in May or early in June, the blue nights had been just making their appearance. I had first noticed them not long after she was admitted to the ICU, which happened to be in the Greenberg Pavilion. In the lobby of the Greenberg Pavilion there hung portraits of its major benefactors, the most prominent of whom had played founding roles in the insurance conglomerate AIG and so had figured in news stories about the AIG bailout. During the first weeks I had reason to visit the ICU in the Greenberg Pavilion I was startled by the familiarity of these faces in the portraits, and, in the early evening, when I came downstairs from the ICU, would pause to study them. Then I would walk out into the increasingly intense blue of that time of day in that early summer season.

This routine seemed for a while to bring luck.

It was a period when the doctors in the ICU did not seem uniformly discouraging.

It was a period when improvement seemed possible.

There was even mention of a step-down unit, although the step-down unit never exactly materialized.

Then one night, leaving the ICU and pausing as

usual by the AIG portraits, I realized: there would be no step-down unit.

The light outside had already changed.

The light outside was no longer blue.

She had so far since entering this ICU undergone five surgical interventions. She had remained ventilated and sedated throughout. The original surgical incision had never been closed. I had asked her surgeon how long he could continue doing this. He had mentioned a surgeon at Cornell who had done eighteen such interventions on a single patient.

"And that patient lived," the surgeon had said.

In what condition, I had asked.

"Your daughter wasn't in great condition when she arrived here," the surgeon had said.

So that was where we were. The light outside was already darkening. The summer was already ending and she was still upstairs in the ICU overlooking the river and the surgeon was saying she wasn't in great condition when they put her there.

In other words she was dying.

I now knew she was dying.

There was now no way to avoid knowing it. There would now be no way to believe the doctors when they tried not to seem discouraging. There would now be no way to pretend to myself that the spirit of the AIG founders would pull this one out. She would die. She would not necessarily die that night, she would not necessarily die the next day, but we were now on track to the day she would die.

August 26 was the day she would die.

August 26 was the day Gerry and I would leave the ICU overlooking the river and walk into Central Park.

I see as I write this that there is no uniformity in the way I refer to Gerry. Sometimes I call him "Gerry," sometimes I call him "her husband." She liked the sound of that. *Her husband. My husband.*

She would say it again and again.

When she could still speak.

Which, as the days continued to shorten and the track to narrow, was by no means every day.

You notice we're doing hand compression.

Because the patient could no longer get enough oxygen through the vent.

For at least an hour now.

In an underpass beneath one of the bridges in Central Park that day someone was playing a saxophone. I do not remember what song he was playing but I remember that it was torchy and I remember stopping under the bridge, turning aside, eyes on the fading leaves, unable to hold back tears.

"The power of cheap music," Gerry said, or maybe I only thought it.

Gerry. Her husband.

The day she cut the peach-colored cake from Payard.
The day she wore the shoes with the bright-red soles.
The day the plumeria tattoo showed through her veil.
In fact I was not even crying for the saxophone.

I was crying for the tiles, the Minton tiles in the arcade south of Bethesda Fountain, Sara Mankiewicz's pattern, Quintana's christening. I was crying for Connie Wald walking her dog through Boulder City and across Hoover Dam. I was crying for Diana holding the champagne flute and smoking the cigarette in Sara Mankiewicz's living room. I was crying for Diana who had talked to Blake Watson so that I could bring the beautiful baby girl he had delivered home from the nursery at St. John's Hospital in Santa Monica.

Diana who would die in the ICU at Cedars in Los Angeles.

Dominique who would die in the ICU at Cedars in Los Angeles.

The beautiful baby girl who would die in the ICU in the Greenberg Pavilion at New York Cornell.

You notice we're doing hand compression.

Because the patient can no longer get enough oxygen through the vent.

For at least an hour now.

Like when someone dies, don't dwell on it.

30

Six weeks after she died we had a service for her, at the Dominican Church of St. Vincent Ferrer on Lexington Avenue. Gregorian chant was sung. A movement from Schubert's Piano Sonata in B-flat was played. Her cousin Griffin read a few paragraphs John had written about her in *Quintana & Friends:* "Quintana will be eleven this week. She approaches adolescence with what I can only describe as panache, but then watching her journey from infancy has always been like watching Sandy Koufax pitch or Bill Russell play basketball." Her cousin Kelley read a poem she had written as a child in Malibu about the Santa Ana winds:

> *Gardens are dead*
> *Animals not fed*
> *Flowers don't smell*

Dry is the well
People's careers slide right down
Brain in the pan turns around
People mumble as leaves crumble
Fire ashes tumble.

Susan Traylor, her best friend since they met at nursery school in Malibu, read a letter from her. Calvin Trillin spoke about her. Gerry read a Galway Kinnell poem that she had liked, Patti Smith sang her a lullaby that she had written for her own son. I read the poems by Wallace Stevens and T. S. Eliot, "Domination of Black" and "New Hampshire," with which I had put her to sleep when she was a baby. "Do the peacocks," she would say once she could talk. "Do the peacocks," or "do the apple trees."

"Domination of Black" had peacocks in it.

"New Hampshire" had apple trees in it.

I think of "Domination of Black" every time I see the peacocks at St. John the Divine.

I did the peacocks that day at St. Vincent Ferrer.

I did the apple trees.

The following day her husband and my brother and his family and Griffin and his father and I went up to St. John the Divine and placed her ashes in a marble wall in St. Ansgar's Chapel along with those of my mother and John.

My mother's name was already on the marble wall at St. John the Divine.

EDUENE JERRETT DIDION

MAY 30 1910—MAY 15 2001

John's name was already on it.

JOHN GREGORY DUNNE

MAY 25 1932—DECEMBER 30 2003

There had been two spaces remaining, the names not yet engraved.

Now there was one.

During the month or so after placing first my mother's and then John's ashes in the wall at St. John the Divine I had the same dream, repeated again and again. In the dream it was always six in the afternoon, the hour at which the evensong bells are rung and the cathedral doors are closed and locked.

In the dream I hear the six o'clock bells.

In the dream I see the cathedral darkening, the doors locking.

You can imagine the dream from there.

When I left the cathedral after placing her ashes in the marble wall I avoided thinking about the dream.

I promised myself that I would maintain momentum.

"Maintain momentum" was the imperative that echoed all the way downtown.

In fact I had no idea what would happen if I lost it.

In fact I had no idea what it was.

I assumed, incorrectly, that it had something to do with movement, traveling, checking in and out of hotels, going to and from the airport.

I tried this.

A week after placing the ashes in the wall at St. John the Divine, I flew to Boston and back to New York and then to Dallas and back to New York and then to Minneapolis and back to New York, doing promotion for *The Year of Magical Thinking*. The following week, again doing promotion and still under the misapprehension that momentum was about traveling, I flew to Washington and back and then to San Francisco and Los Angeles and Denver and Seattle and Chicago and Toronto and finally to Palm Springs, where I was to spend Thanksgiving with my brother and his family. From various points on this itinerary, over the course of which I began to grasp that just going to and from the airport might be insufficient, that some further effort might be required, I spoke by telephone to Scott Rudin, and agreed that I should write and he should produce and David Hare should direct a one-character play, intended for Broadway, based on *The Year of Magical Thinking*.

The three of us, Scott, David, and I, met for the first time on this project a month after Christmas.

A week before Easter, in a tiny theater on West Forty-second Street, we watched the first readings of the play.

A year later it opened, starring Vanessa Redgrave in its single role, at the Booth Theater on West Forty-fifth Street.

As ways of maintaining momentum go this one turned out to be better than most: I remember liking the entire process a good deal. I liked the quiet afternoons backstage with the stage managers and electricians, I liked the way the ushers gathered for instructions downstairs just before the half-hour call. I liked the presence of Shubert security outside, I liked the weight of the stage door as I opened it against the wind through Shubert Alley, l liked the secret passages to and from the stage. I liked that Amanda, who ran the stage door at night, kept on her desk a tin of the cookies she baked. I liked that

Lauri, who managed the Booth for the Shubert Organi-
zation and was doing graduate work in medieval liter-
ature, became our ultimate authority on a few lines
in the play that involved Gawain. I liked the fried
chicken and cornbread and potato salad and greens
we brought in from Piece o' Chicken, a kitchen store-
front near Ninth Avenue. I liked the matzo-ball soup
we brought in from the Hotel Edison coffee shop. I
liked the place to sit we set up backstage, the little
improvised table with the checked tablecloth and
the electrified candle and the menu that read "Café
Didion."

I liked watching the performance from a balcony
above the lights.

I liked being up there alone with the lights and the
play.

I liked it all, but most of all I liked the fact that
although the play was entirely focused on Quintana
there were, five evenings and two afternoons a week,
these ninety full minutes, the run time of the play, during which she did not need to be dead.

During which the question remained open.

During which the denouement had yet to play out.

During which the last scene played did not necessarily need to be played in the ICU overlooking the
East River.

During which the bells would not necessarily sound and the doors would not necessarily be locked at six.

During which the last dialogue heard did not necessarily need to concern the vent.

Like when someone dies, don't dwell on it.

31

O n the evening late in August when the play closed
Vanessa took the yellow roses provided for her
curtain calls and laid them on the stage, beneath the
photograph of John and Quintana on the deck in Malibu that was the closing drop of the set Bob Crowley
had designed for the production.

The theater cleared.

I was gratified to see how slowly it cleared, as if the
audience shared my wish not to leave John and Quintana alone.

We stood in the wings and drank champagne.

Before I left that evening someone pointed out the
yellow roses Vanessa had laid on the stage floor and
asked if I wanted to take them.

I did not want to take the yellow roses.

I did not want the yellow roses touched.

I wanted the yellow roses right there, where Vanessa

had left them, with John and Quintana on the stage of the Booth, lying there on the stage all night, lit only by the ghost light, still there on the stage right down to the inevitable instant of the morning's eight-a.m. load-out. *"Performance 144 + 23 Previews + 1 Actors Fund,"* the stage manager's performance notes read for that night. *"Magical evening. Lovely final show. Call from the director pre-show. Roses at the call. Champagne toast. Guests included Griffin Dunne and daughter Hannah and Marian Seldes. Café Didion served up its final Piece o' Chicken and sides."* By that evening when the play closed it seemed clear that I had in fact maintained momentum, but it also seemed clear that maintaining momentum had been at a certain cost. This cost had always been predictable but I only that night began to put it into words. One phrase that came to mind that night was "pushing yourself." Another was "beyond endurance."

32

"I fell prey to water intoxication or low sodium, which is characterized by hallucination, memory loss, and corporeal ineptness; a veritable cornucopia of psychoses. I could hear voices, see four different images on the television at one time, read a book in which each word cd separate to fill the page. I'd ask people on the phone who they thought they were talking to cause i certainly didn't know. & I fell constantly. On top of this phantasmagoric experience, I had a stroke." So wrote the playwright Ntozake Shange, in *In the Fullness of Time: 32 Women on Life After 50*, about the maladies that struck her from the blue in her fifties. "The stroke put an end to nanoseconds of images & left a body with diminished vision, no strength, immobile legs, slurred speech, and no recollection of how to read."

She learned to remember how to read.

She learned to remember how to write.

She learned to remember how to walk, how to talk.

She became the person Quintana dreamed of becoming, the person who, by *not dwelling on it,* wakes one morning and finds her revised circumstances corrected. "I am not dead, I am older," she tells us from this improved perspective. "But I can still memorize a stanza or two. What I have memorized is my child's face at different points in her life."

33

Ill health, which is another way of describing what it can cost to maintain momentum, overtakes us when we can imagine no reason to expect it. I can tell you to the hour when it overtook me—a Thursday morning, August 2, 2007—when I woke with what seemed to be an earache and a reddened area on my face that I mistook for a staph infection.

I remember thinking of this as trying, time-consuming, the waste of a morning I could not afford.

Because I had what I mistook for an earache I would need that morning to see an otolaryngologist.

Because I had what I mistook for a staph infection I would need that morning to see a dermatologist.

Before noon I had been diagnosed: not an earache, not a staph infection, but herpes zoster, shingles, an inflammation of the nervous system, an adult recurrence, generally thought to have been triggered or heightened by stress, of the virus responsible for childhood chickenpox.

"Shingles": it sounded minor, even mildly comical, something about which a great-aunt might complain, or an elderly neighbor; an amusing story tomorrow.

Tomorrow. When I will be fine. Restored. Well.

Telling the amusing story.

You'll never guess what it turned out to be. "Shingles," imagine.

Nothing to worry about then, I remember saying to the doctor who made the diagnosis.

Zoster can be a pretty nasty virus, the doctor said, guarded.

Still in the mode for maintaining momentum, and still oblivious to the extent to which maintaining momentum was precisely what had led me to the doctor's office, I did not ask in what ways zoster could be a pretty nasty virus.

Instead I went home, smoothed some translucent foundation over what had now been established as not a staph infection, took one of the antiviral tablets the doctor had given me, and left for West Forty-fifth Street. I left for West Forty-fifth Street not because I felt any better (in fact I felt worse) but because going to the theater had been my plan for the day, going to the theater was that day's momentum: get to the Booth in time for the 3:30 understudy rehearsal, walk across

West Forty-fifth Street during the break and pick up fried chicken and greens to eat backstage, stay for the performance and have a drink afterwards with Vanessa and whoever else was around. *"Direct, engaging, well-tempered,"* the stage manager's performance notes for the evening read. *"Ms. Redgrave nervous pre-show. Vortex very clear. Rapt audience. Cell phone at very top of show. In attendance: Joan Didion (piece o' chicken at the café, show, and ladies' cocktail hour). Hot humid day; stage temp: comfortable."*

I have no memory of Ms. Redgrave nervous pre-show.

I have no memory of the ladies' cocktail hour. I am told that it featured daiquiris, blended backstage by Vanessa's dresser, and that I had one.

I remember only that the hot humid day with the comfortable stage temperature was followed, for me, by a week of 103-degree fever, three weeks of acute pain in the nerves on the left side of my head and face (including, inconveniently, those nerves that trigger headaches, earaches, and toothaches), and after that by a condition the neurologist described as "postviral ataxia" but I could describe only as "not knowing where my body starts and stops."

I can only think that this may have been what Ntozake Shange meant by "corporeal ineptness."

I no longer had any balance.

I dropped whatever I tried to pick up.

I could not tie my shoes, I could not button a sweater or clip my hair off my face, the simplest acts of fastening and unfastening were now beyond me.

I could no longer catch a ball.

I mention the ball only because (I do not in fact normally catch balls during the course of the day) the single accurate description I would hear or read of these symptoms I was just then beginning to experience was that provided by a professional tennis player, James Blake, who, after a season of considerable stress—he had fractured a vertebra in his neck before the French Open and by the time he was healing his father was dying—woke one morning in his early twenties with similar symptoms. "Instantly, I realized just how many things were wrong," he later wrote, in *Breaking Back: How I Lost Everything and Won Back My Life,* about his initial attempt to return to what had been his life. "Not only was my balance off, but my vision was messed up as well—I had a hard time tracking the ball from Brian's and Evan's rackets to my own. I could see them hit it, I'd sort of lose it for a moment, then suddenly it would register much closer to me. This was especially disconcerting because neither Brian nor Evan hit anywhere near as hard as the average tour player."

He tries to run right for a shot, and finds that his coordination has gone wherever his vision went.

He tries to volley, just hit a few balls, and finds that the balls now hit him.

He asks the neurotologist to whom he has been referred at Yale–New Haven how long he should expect these symptoms to last.

"At least three months," the neurotologist says. "Or it could take four years."

This is not what the professional tennis player wants to hear, nor is it what I want to hear.

Still.

I maintain faith (another word for momentum) that my own symptoms, which have continued to recur in slightly altered incarnations and have so far lasted closer to four years than to three months, will improve, lessen, even resolve.

I do what I can to encourage this resolution, I follow instructions.

I regularly report to Sixtieth and Madison for physical therapy.

I keep the freezer stocked with Maison du Chocolat vanilla ice cream.

I collect encouraging news, even focus on it.

For example:

James Blake has since returned to the tour. I fix on this fact.

Meanwhile, like Ntozake Shange, I memorize my child's face.

34

I find myself studying, in a copy of *The New York Review of Books,* a Magnum photograph of Sophia Loren taken during a Christian Dior fashion show in Paris in 1968. In this photograph Sophia Loren is sitting on a gilt chair, wearing a silk turban and smoking a cigarette, achingly polished, forever soignée as she watches "the bride," the traditional end of the show. It occurs to me that this Magnum photograph would have been taken not long after Sophia Loren herself had been "the bride," in fact twice the bride, married in France to Carlo Ponti for the second time after the annulment of their original Mexican marriage, the marriage for which he had been charged with bigamy and threatened with excommunication in Italy.

A "scandal" of the time.

It has become hard to remember how reliably "scandal" once came our way.

Elizabeth Taylor and Richard Burton, a scandal.

Ingrid Bergman and Roberto Rossellini, a scandal.

Sophia Loren and Carlo Ponti, a scandal.

I continue studying the photograph.

I imagine the object of this particular scandal leaving Dior and going to lunch in the courtyard of the Plaza Athénée.

I imagine her sitting with Carlo Ponti in the courtyard, eating an éclair with a fork, the vines that line the courtyard blowing slightly, ivy, *lierre,* sunlight glowing pink through the red canvas canopies over the windows. I imagine the sound of the little birds that flock in the *lierre,* a twittering, a constant presence and an occasional—when, say, a metal shutter is opened, or when, say, Sophia Loren rises from her table to cross the courtyard—swelling of birdsong.

I imagine her leaving the Plaza Athénée, photographers flashing around her as she slides into a waiting car on the Avenue Montaigne.

The cigarette, the silk turban.

It strikes me that she looks in this photograph not unlike the women in the photographs Nick took at Quintana's christening.

Quintana's christening was in 1966, this Christian Dior show was two years later, 1968: 1966 and 1968 were a world removed from each other in the political and cultural life of the United States but they were for women who presented themselves a certain way the same time. It was a way of looking, it was a way of being. It was a period. What became of that way of looking, that way of being, that time, that period? What became of the women smoking cigarettes in their Chanel suits and their David Webb bracelets, what became of Diana holding the champagne flute and one of Sara Mankiewicz's Minton plates? What became of Sara Mankiewicz's Minton plates? What became of the clay tennis court at the house on Franklin Avenue in Hollywood, the court I watched Quintana weed on her fat baby knees? What gave Quintana the idea that weeding a court on which no one ever played—even the net was down, punched through during years of neglect, dragging in the weeds and the dust that got scuffed off the clay—was a necessary task, her assignment, her duty? Was weeding the unused tennis court at the house on Franklin Avenue something like equipping the projection room in the doll's house in Malibu? Was weeding the unused tennis court something like writing a novel? Was it one more way of assuming an adult role? Why did she so need to assume an adult role? Whatever became of those fat baby knees, whatever became of Bunny Rabbit?

As it happens I know what became of Bunny Rabbit.

She left Bunny Rabbit in a suite at the Royal Hawaiian Hotel in Honolulu.

I learned this halfway across the Pacific, when she was sitting next to me in the darkened upstairs cabin on the evening Pan Am flight back to Los Angeles.

There was still a Pan Am then.

There was still a TWA then.

There was still a Pan Am and there was still a TWA and Bendel's was still on West Fifty-seventh Street and it still had Holly's Harp chiffons and lettuce edges and sizes zero and two.

Sitting next to me on that evening flight back to Los Angeles my child mourned Bunny Rabbit's cruel fate: Bunny Rabbit was lost, Bunny Rabbit was left behind, Bunny Rabbit had been abandoned. Yet by the time we taxied into the gate at LAX she had successfully translated Bunny Rabbit's cruel fate into Bunny Rabbit's good luck: the Royal Hawaiian, the suite, the room-service breakfasts. Where did the morning went. The white sand, the swimming pool. Walking to the reef. Swimming off the raft. Bunny Rabbit was even now, we could be certain, swimming off the raft.

Swim off the raft, walk to the reef.

Imagine a five-year-old walking to the reef.

Like when someone dies, don't dwell on it.

How could I not still need that child with me?

I feel impelled to locate, by way of establishing at least one survivor of the period, a recent photograph of Sophia Loren.

I type her name into Google Images.

I find such a photograph: Sophia Loren arriving at some kind of publicity event, one of those red-carpet arrivals during which the PR people hover close, alerting the photographers to the approach of the celebrity. As I check the caption on the photograph I notice in passing that Sophia Loren was born in 1934, the same year in which I myself was born. I am spellbound: Sophia Loren, too, is seventy-five years old. Sophia Loren is seventy-five years old and no one on that red carpet, to my knowledge, is yet suggesting that she is making an inadequate adjustment to aging. This entirely meaningless discovery floods me with restored hope, a revived sense of the possible.

35

When we lose that sense of the possible we lose it fast.

One day we are absorbed by dressing well, following the news, keeping up, coping, what we might call *staying alive;* the next day we are not. One day we are turning the pages of whatever has arrived in the day's mail with real enthusiasm—maybe it is *Vogue,* maybe it is *Foreign Affairs,* whatever it is we are intensely interested, pleased to have this handbook to *keeping up,* this key to *staying alive*—yet the next day we are walking uptown on Madison past Barney's and Armani or on Park past the Council on Foreign Relations and we are not even glancing at their windows. One day we are looking at the Magnum photograph of Sophia Loren at the Christian Dior show in Paris in 1968 and thinking yes, it could be me, I could wear that dress, I was in Paris that year; a blink of the eye later we are in

one or another doctor's office being told what has
already gone wrong, why we will never again wear the
red suede sandals with the four-inch heels, never
again wear the gold hoop earrings, the enameled
beads, never now wear the dress Sophia Loren is wearing. The sun damage inflicted when we swam off the
raft in our twenties against all advice is only now surfacing (we were told not to burn, we were told what
would happen, we were told to wear sunscreen, we
ignored all warnings): melanoma, squamous cell, long
hours now spent watching the dermatologist carve out
the carcinomas with the names we do not want to hear.

Long hours now spent getting the intravenous infu-
sions of the medication that promises to replace the
bone lost to aging.

Long hours now spent getting the intravenous infu-
sions and wondering why the Vitamin D we thought we
were accumulating by not wearing sunscreen failed to
realize its bone-building potential.

Long hours now spent waiting for the scans, waiting
for the EEGs, sitting in frigid waiting rooms turning
the pages of *The Wall Street Journal* and *AARP The
Magazine* and *Neurology Today* and the alumnae magazines of the Columbia and Cornell medical schools.

Sitting in frigid waiting rooms once again produc-
ing the insurance cards, once again explaining why,
the provider's preference notwithstanding, the Writers

Guild-Industry Health Plan needs to be the primary and Medicare the secondary, not, despite my age—my age is now an issue in every waiting room—vice versa.

Sitting in frigid waiting rooms once again filling out the New York–Presbyterian questionnaires.

Sitting in frigid waiting rooms once again listing the medications and the symptoms and the descriptions and dates of previous hospitalizations: just make up the dates, just take a guess and stand by it, for some reason "1982" always comes to mind, *well, fine, "1982" it is, "1982" will have to do,* there can be no way to get the answer to this question right.

Sitting in frigid waiting rooms trying to think of the name and telephone number of the person I want notified in case of emergency.

Whole days now spent on this one question, this question with no possible answer: *who do I want notified in case of emergency?*

I think it over. I do not want even to consider "in case of emergency."

Emergency, I continue to believe, is what happens to someone else.

I say that I continue to believe this even as I know that I do not.

I mean, think back: what about that business with the folding metal chair in the rehearsal room on West Forty-second Street? What exactly was I afraid of there? What did I fear in that rehearsal room if not an "emergency"? Or what about walking home after an early dinner on Third Avenue and waking up in a pool of blood on my own bedroom floor? Might not waking up in a pool of blood on my own bedroom floor qualify as an "emergency"?

All right. Accepted. "In case of emergency" could apply.

Who to notify. I try harder.

Still, no name comes to mind.

I could give the name of my brother, but my brother lives three thousand miles from what might be defined in New York as an emergency. I could give Griffin's name, but Griffin is shooting a picture. Griffin is on location. Griffin is sitting in the dining room of one or another Hilton Inn—a few too many people at the table, a little too much noise—and Griffin is not picking up his cell. I could give the name of which- ever close friend in New York comes first to mind, but the close friend in New York who comes first to mind is actually, on reflection, not even in New York, out of town, out of the country, away, certainly unreachable in the best case, possibly unwilling in the worst.

As I consider the word "unwilling" my lagging cog- nition kicks in.

The familiar phrase "need to know" surfaces.

The phrase "need to know" has been the problem all along.

Only one person needs to know.

She is of course the one person who needs to know.

Let me just be in the ground.

Let me just be in the ground and go to sleep.

I imagine telling her.

I am able to imagine telling her because I still see her.

Hello, Mommies.

The same way I still see her weeding the clay court on Franklin Avenue.

The same way I still see her sitting on the bare floor crooning back to the eight-track.

Do you wanna dance. I wanna dance.

The same way I still see the stephanotis in her braid, the same way I still see the plumeria tattoo through her veil. The same way I still see the bright-red soles on her shoes as she kneels at the altar. The same way I still see her, in the darkened upstairs cabin on the evening Pan Am from Honolulu to LAX, inventing the unforeseen uptick in Bunny Rabbit's fortunes.

I know that I can no longer reach her.

I know that, should I try to reach her—should I take her hand as if she were again sitting next to me in the upstairs cabin on the evening Pan Am from Honolulu to LAX, should I lull her to sleep against my shoulder, should I sing her the song about Daddy gone to get the rabbit skin to wrap his baby bunny in—she will fade from my touch.

Vanish.

Pass into nothingness: the Keats line that frightened her.

Fade as the blue nights fade, go as the brightness goes.

Go back into the blue.

I myself placed her ashes in the wall.

I myself saw the cathedral doors locked at six.

I know what it is I am now experiencing.

I know what the frailty is, I know what the fear is.

The fear is not for what is lost.

What is lost is already in the wall.

What is lost is already behind the locked doors.

The fear is for what is still to be lost.

You may see nothing still to be lost.

Yet there is no day in her life on which I do not see her.

A NOTE ON THE TYPE

This book was set in Bodoni, a typeface named after Giambattista Bodoni (1740–1813), the celebrated printer and type designer of Parma. Bodoni's innovations in type style included a greater degree of contrast in the thick and thin elements of the letters and a sharper and more angular finish of details.

TYPESET BY

Scribe, Philadelphia, Pennsylvania

PRINTED AND BOUND BY

RR Donnelley, Harrisonburg, Virginia

DESIGNED BY

Iris Weinstein